SOUL
{control}

SOUL

{control}

[will]

emotions]

[mind]

Whoever Controls Your Soul
{controls your destiny}

BY

MAC HAMMOND

Soul Control
Whoever Controls Your Soul Controls Your Destiny

ISBN 1-57399-364-6

First printing, March 2007

© 2007 Mac Hammond

Mac Hammond Ministries

Published by Mac Hammond Ministries
PO Box 29469
Minneapolis, MN 55429

Contents

I want.

Chapter 9
I Want It. And I Want It Now!.

Chapter 10
Supernatural Pressure Relief

Chapter 11
Your Supernatural Source of Comfort

Section 2—The Body

Chapter 12
Body Language—What's Yours Saying?

Chapter 13
Who's Really in Charge?
The Real You—or Your Body?

Section 3 —The Spirit

Chapter 14
Finally! The Real You

Chapter 15
The Foundational Key to a Spirit-Controlled Life

Chapter 16
Never Look Back

Chapter 17
Follow the Fire

Chapter 18
Be Filled With the Spirit

Soul Control —
It Determines Your Destiny

Chapter 1

Imagine always hearing the voice of God and following it accurately.

Imagine a life where you don't make disastrous decisions or take wrong turns.

Imagine a life filled with all the goodness of God.

Does it sound too good to be true? It doesn't have to be. In fact, as you learn to control your soul properly, you can have a life as described above!

But what is soul control and where does it start?

It begins with our decisions.

Each day we make a myriad of decisions and choices. Many are conscious and deliberate while others are subconscious based on our preconditioning. Yet according to Deuteronomy 28, every single choice falls into one of two categories: life and blessing or death and cursing.

In other words, the life you have right now and whether it is full of blessing or cursing is a result of choices you have made. Many don't like to hear this as they like to play the blame game and make excuses for the quality of their lives. But the Bible is clear: your life is a product of the choices *you* have made. Thus, understanding how to make right choices is critical and the process must be understood.

Decision making is the consummation of the operation of your soul, and in short, that's what your soul exists to do. Make decisions. Your soul consists of the mind, the emotions, and the will. When you make decisions, or choices, you exercise your will on the basis of the interaction between your mind and your emotions.

Intellectually, you absorb and evaluate all of the information that comes to you through your sensory perceptions, what you see, hear, touch, taste, and feel. Then emotionally, you feel things about certain situations and certain circumstances. Based on the interaction between your intellectual evaluation and your emotional response, you make a choice. You enact your will and you choose.

Decision making and making choices is the final consummation of all God intended your soulish realm to do. As a result, what you consistently choose depends on whom or what controls your soul. In other words, whoever controls your soul controls your destiny—be it God, Satan, religious tradition, circumstances, your flesh, or other people.

Obviously, God wants to control your soul and determine your destiny—but not directly. He wants *you* to train your soul to be in subjection to your spirit, so you can live a truly Spirit-led life. In other words, if the Holy Spirit, through your spirit, can control your soul, then the will of God will be your destiny.

Most of the time, the operation of your soul is on a subconscious level. It just happens and you're not really aware of it. The purpose of this chapter is to begin to make you aware of it so you can exercise some control in the process.

All three parts of your soul interact with one another. It's the place where what you think (the mind) interacts with what you feel (your emotions) and the result is a choice to act (your will). In other words, when your ability to think interacts with your feelings, they produce a desire—and desire always precedes decision.

The most consistent decisions you make in a particular area are a product of the strongest desire you have regarding that area of your life. In other words, you won't have strong desire and then make decisions opposite to that desire. That's not the way you were created to function. So, on a regular basis, when what you think interacts with what you feel, whichever between the two is most dominant usually determines your decision. And thus, whatever is the dominant influence over your thoughts and feelings is controlling your decision-making process.

Here's an example of what I'm explaining. Suppose I feel a lot of anger, irritation, and aggravation toward someone. Perhaps they've hurt me recently, and I still feel some feelings of unforgiveness toward them. I don't really want to be around them. I don't feel friendly toward them. Yet, because I'm a believer, and I have enough of the Word in my mind, I think, *Well, I need to show myself friendly. I need to be gentle and kind. I need to have a soft answer. I need to believe the best. I need to expect them to respond to me.*

Whichever part of me is most dominate—my mind or my emotions—and whatever input is driving that dominance will determine how I behave toward the other person. Your mind is the logical part of you that has the capacity to weigh, measure, evaluate information, and come to a conclusion. Your emotions are where you feel. If you have thought more about your bad feelings than about what the Word of God instructs you to do, even though you know better, your strong ill feelings will dominate your behavior. Despite your good intentions, you will make a choice for death.

Another example is how you might feel when you're overly tired. You feel like you would love to sleep for another two hours. You feel like it would be nice to stay in bed. But your mind starts thinking, *That would really tick off my supervisor. It might cost me a raise. Worst case scenario, it might cost me my job.* So the desire to keep your job is stronger than your feelings of how nice it would be to stay in bed. So you make a decision for life and you get out of bed.

My point is for you to see how the soul works and to recognize that God created you to function this way. Whichever part of you is strongest and most influential will control you. Unfortunately, many people never understand this and thus they refuse to engage their minds into the equation of being saved.

THE ROLE OF YOUR MIND

A vast majority of Christians feed on spiritual information and good Bible teaching, but they don't engage their brains or understand the role of their minds. They seemingly "check out." The end result is that they become "religious." That means they can quote the Bible backward and forward, but they have no understanding of its meaning. Somehow, they have missed God's intention for how their souls are to operate in the kingdom of God.

God wants you to use your brain to understand the Word of God. Your mind, which is an integral part of your soul, has the God-given capacity to perceive, to understand, to rationalize, and come to logical conclusions. It's created to fulfill these God-ordained processes.

So whether you are aware of it or not, your current quality of life is a direct result of what you have been doing with your mind. Why is this so important to grasp? Because daily decisions ultimately determine your quality of life and when the mind is not being fed the proper information, decisions for life and blessing are not going to happen!

THE ROLE OF YOUR EMOTIONS

Where do our emotions come into play? Emotions are designed by God to give us the momentum and impetus toward the things we've decided to do. They are the part of us that have the capacity to feel. They are the result of what we have meditated upon. Know this, what you consistently think about and the words you speak ultimately direct what you feel emotionally.

God wants us to feel excitement, enthusiasm, and determination about what He's called us to do. To feel that way, we have to meditate—think—about God's plans, purposes, and power. When we do, the capacity of our emotions produces momentum in that direction of our God-given destiny.

So, the soulish operation should function this way. You are constantly receiving data—input from your spirit and your body that you are weighing, measuring, evaluating, and esteeming. You should then make decisions that you believe are consistent with the will of God—what you believe is best for you. As you meditate on those decisions and get emotionally stirred about them, a momentum builds that moves you in that direction.

But in an uncontrolled soul, a person thinks and acts out of the natural arena because it is more dominant. They react to what they can see, feel, and taste. They give more credibility to the natural consideration. When thoughts come, they don't try to control them. They don't practice 2 Corinthians 10:5 which says:

Casting down imaginations, and every high thing that exalteth itself against the knowledge of God, and bringing into captivity every thought to the obedience of Christ.

They don't cast down wrong thoughts or vain imaginations. Rather, they let the random rush of thoughts generated mostly by the world in which we live dominate their thinking.

The result is a life dominated by information from the carnal arena—a life of decisions dominated by wrong information and feelings.

The painful result is believers who have an excess of worldly information, but want to make choices according to God's will.

Their paths are rocky because they can't make the right choices. They don't have enough input of the right information and an overload of the wrong information.

Oftentimes a Christian will say to me, "God told me to do this. I *know* God told me to do this. I got it strong." But the truth is he or she doesn't have enough of the right information to discern between what's of God and what's not of God.

DIVIDING YOUR SPIRIT AND SOUL

So in summary, the kingdom of darkness works hard to influence your decisions through your body—through your sensory perceptions, natural carnal reasoning process, circumstances, and unwitting people.

God works to influence you through your spirit by His Word and the Holy Spirit. And it's your soul that's in the middle. It's the part of you where your spirit and your body have their primary channels of expression.

The key to how you live your life on this earth, the key to how you will live after you depart this earth, the nature and shape of your eternal destiny, depends on who is controlling your soul—that powerful part of you that encompasses your mind, will, and emotions.

If Satan controls your soul, then he determines your destiny.

If people in your life control your soul—people who the enemy uses to provoke anger, engage your emotional response, or stir you up any way they can and empower you to generate negative thoughts, resentment, and bitterness—then they determine your destiny.

But if God controls your soul, then He will determine your destiny.

THE SOUL
{section 1}

I think.

The Law of the Mind

{Chapter 2}

The Bible clearly and consistently promotes "faith" as the power source for changing the circumstance of your life. Yet there are other factors which must be mixed with your faith for it to fully produce what God intends, including your behavior.

James 2:17 says faith without works is dead. In other words, if your behavior (or what *The Amplified Bible* calls "corresponding actions" in this passage) does not line up with the things you believe, your faith dies unborn.

But if your behavior is in line with your heart's belief, power is released to change your circumstance. So behavior is incredibly important in receiving the blessing of God. And ultimately, behavior is determined by the decision-making process of the soul which operates under *the law of the mind.*

In Romans 7:22 Paul says, "I delight in the law of God according to the inward man..." And then in verse 23 he says this; "But I see another law in my members, warring against *the law of my mind,* and bringing me into captivity to the law of sin which is in my members" (NKJV).

The apostle Paul, inspired by the Holy Spirit, is pointing out the conflict that every Christian experiences. We hear and believe God's Word, and we delight in it inwardly. Yet other influences are seeking to work through our flesh and limit the fruit-bearing potential of the seed that has been planted in our hearts.

The battle is waged in the realm of the soul, specifically the mind. And your ability to operate the law of the mind properly will determine whether God dictates the quality of your life or whether the law of sin and death operating through your members dictates the quality of your life.

The Bible reveals this truth in many different ways. In Proverbs 23:7, the Spirit of God puts it this way; "For as he [mankind] thinketh in his heart, so he is." This is another way of saying what I've just said to you; ultimately, your behavior and the quality of your life are going to be a product of how you think or what you think on most.

HOW THE MIND OPERATES

It's important to understand that your mind works by mental imagery, meaning you don't think in words, you think in images. For example, if I said to you the words "yellow dog," you wouldn't see in your mind the letters y-e-l-l-o-w d-o-g. You would see a yellow dog—a picture, a mental image. That's the way the mind functions.

These building blocks of mental images form a picture of your perception of reality which is the operation of the imagination, and imagination is what produces behavior. So the law of the mind could be stated this way: all consistent behavior is rooted in your perception of reality, which is formed by whatever ingrained mental images you have stored in your imagination.

It is important to realize this law is true whether what you are trying to achieve is good or bad. Just like gravity, a law is a law and it works regardless of the circumstances or who is involved. In other words, the law of the mind is always at work whether a person realizes it or not. When operated as God intends, the law of the mind will bring forth behavior in line with the Word sown in your heart.

REACTIVE BEHAVIOR

Of course, some behavior is reactive and is simply an emotional response to a stimulus of the moment. But all consistent behavior (or patterned behavior) is rooted in the imagination. In fact, your patterns of response to any external stimuli are dependant upon your mental conditioning or programming in the earlier years of your life.

At the very earliest age, you begin cataloging data through the process of mental programming or conditioning. As time passes, your mind produces automatic responses to various stimuli without you even consciously thinking about it. This ability to establish patterns of response without having to stop and think through everything is designed by God for our good.

Most behavioral scientists agree that the first 15 or 20 years of human life is when most of this mental conditioning takes place. The people that influence you the most in this process are those who have the greatest exposure to you during these formative years. This is why your parents or whoever had the closest contact with you during this time have more to do with how you think (and thus your current behavior) than anyone else. Others, like teachers and friends, have input in this process as well.

But the basic point I'm trying to make is that this early conditioning and programming establishes unconscious thought processes that will dictate the way you respond to things later in life. So when we talk about soul control and the law of the mind, we are not just focusing on the conscious thoughts of the moment, we are also focusing on the earlier programming that took place in the formative years of your life. If you are going to experience lasting change in any area of your life, this arena cannot be ignored.

THE SPIRIT OF THE MIND

The apostle Paul calls this arena the "spirit of your mind." Ephesians 4:22 says:

Put off, concerning the former conversation [manner of life=behavior] *the old man, which is corrupt according to the deceitful lusts; and be renewed in the spirit of your mind; and that ye put on the new man, which after God is created in righteousness and true holiness.*

Notice it doesn't just say renew your mind. Paul says to be renewed in the "spirit" of your mind. In other words, there is more to exercising proper control over your soul and cooperating with the law of the mind properly than just focusing on the thought of the moment.

The *spirit* of the mind refers to the way we are—the attitudes, the value systems, the things that make us who we are—that give us our patterns of response to whatever may stimulate us. Foundationally, this is what needs to be renewed if we're to experience change.

New mental images in our imagination are what will allow us to put off the old man and put on the new man. As we change the preconditioning (the programming that has taken place in our minds earlier on), our behavior will begin aligning with God's purposes.

IMAGINATION—A VITAL TOOL

We have begun to see the importance of our imagination, yet let's go a little further and see that it also carries with it the supernatural ability to achieve what you imagine. In 1 Peter 1:13, the apostle Peter makes a statement that gives us more insight into this matter:

> *Wherefore gird up the loins of your mind. Be sober* [that means sound minded] *and hope* [or confidently expect, talking about the promise of God] *to the end for the grace that is to be brought unto you at the revelation of Jesus Christ.*

In the first part of this verse, he says "gird up the loins of your mind." The word "loins" fascinates me. If you look it up, it means "the seat of procreative power." Now in a biological sense, our loins are located somewhere else. And it's the way biological life is conceived and brought into this natural arena. So obviously, he's talking about some other kind of life.

God has created your mind with the capacity to bring the life of God into manifestation in this natural arena. When you're born again, the life of God takes up residence on the inside of you. The challenge for the believer then is to turn spiritual truth into temporal truth. Somehow or some way, you have to get the spiritual truth that's on the inside of you out into the natural arena of life—and your mind is the key to making that happen.

Your mind has the power to bring the life that's inside of you out into a natural existence. That's why God refers to it as the loins of your mind. The capacity to produce life in the natural realm is in your mind.

From what we read in Romans chapter 7 and Ephesians chapter 4, we know that if you put the law of the mind to work and be renewed in the spirit of your mind, it will produce the will of God and the life of God. This passage magnifies this truth and communicates that our mind is the seat of that procreative power.

This is also clear in Genesis chapter 11, where the Bible tells of an unregenerate people who didn't know God and didn't have the Spirit of God. But they were doing something God said they could not be restrained from—building the Tower of Babel.

So in verse 6 it says:

Behold, the people is one, and they have all one language; and this they begin to do: and now nothing will be restrained from them, which they have imagined to do.

These people mentally imagined themselves doing something— building the tower—which caused the law of the mind to produce the result of "nothing can restrain them from achieving that."

Once again, we see that *doing* follows *imagining*. But perhaps an even more significant concept is that the imagination carries with it the ability to accomplish and create. These people were not some kind of super race that had something in their minds that we don't have. Yet even in their condition, God said nothing would be restrained from them that they imagined to do.

Clearly, we see that our ability to mentally image and imagine produces behavior and carries with it the supernatural ability to achieve the imagined objective.

We see this validated further in Psalm 2:1:

Why do the heathen rage and the people imagine a vain thing?

Once again, behavior and imagination are connected together. Now obviously, this verse is talking about wrong behavior as the people were *raging* and imagining a *vain* thing. The Hebrew word translated *vain* literally means "empty, worthless, to no purpose." In other words, wrong behavior is a product of using your imagination the wrong way—building a life on mental imagery that is empty, worthless, and to no purpose.

Another important understanding we can gain from this verse is found in the word translated "imagine." It is exactly the same word used in Psalm 1:2 translated "meditate" which is defined as "to ponder, to mutter, to roll it over in your mind." Here we begin to gain more understanding of what is involved in the process of imagining and what you must do to properly renew the spirit of your mind.

A Compelling Case

These scriptures present a compelling case that it doesn't matter if you're born again, Spirit filled, or if you've been going to church for 50 years. If you don't understand how to cooperate as God intends with the law of the mind, then you're not going to experience positive, godly change!

Sadly, this is why a lot of the world looks at Christianity and says, "Man, they're just a bunch of hypocrites." Without controlling the soul as God intends, it's impossible to get rid of the old man and put on the new man who is created in righteousness and true holiness.

But if we choose to cooperate with the law of the mind and learn how to properly renew our minds, we can transform our lives. We can become examples to the world of the power of God!

Renewing Your Mind—
The Foundation

{Chapter 3}

The Bible reveals renewing your mind as the process which releases the significant and supernatural transformation that God desires for your life, like from a caterpillar to a butterfly. Thus, it is really the only way to realize the perfect will of God for your life and fulfill the high calling He has given you.

When God wants to get information to you about His will and calling for you, He accesses your soul through your spirit man, which is indwelt by the Holy Spirit, to impart revelation of His Word and to bring you personal direction for your life.

God's desire is for you to use the information He gives you along with what you gather from the natural arena. He wants you to measure and evaluate your decisions so that you make the right choices.

It sounds so simple. But why is it so hard to accomplish?

Because the soul has to be trained and it isn't your "natural" inclination to do what your born again spirit wants or what the Bible teaches. It's "natural" to do what your body screams for or your feelings tell you. It's "natural" to respond to the information the world and your flesh input into your mind. So the realm of the soul has to be trained—continually.

THE TRAINING PROCESS

The Bible describes the training process this way:

And be not conformed to this world: but be ye transformed by the renewing of your mind, that ye may prove what is that good, and acceptable, and perfect, will of God.

Romans 12:2

The Amplified Bible translates it even more clearly: "Do not be conformed to this world (this age), [fashioned after and adapted to its external, superficial customs], but be transformed (changed) by the [entire] renewal of your mind [by its new ideals and its new attitude], so that you may prove [for yourselves] what is the good and acceptable and perfect will of God, even the thing which is good and acceptable and perfect [in His sight for you]."

To be trained—to be transformed—means your mind has to be renewed.

Romans 12:2 is a familiar verse to most Christians, yet the actual process of renewing the mind and what it entails is not understood as it should be. If it was, we would see a whole lot more Christian butterflies than caterpillars!

Most people think that renewing your mind is defined by simply memorizing Scripture. They think it is doing some internal housecleaning by removing old standards and values and putting in new ones. While that is one way of viewing the process and part of it, it's only a small portion of what renewing the mind is all about.

Renewing isn't just learning or even memorizing Scripture. Renewing means refilling or replenishing. Renewing the mind is taking what you have already learned and doing something with it called refilling and replenishing, which is a continual act. In the same way that faith comes by hearing and hearing and hearing, so does renewing the mind come by renewing and renewing and renewing. It is a continual process of refilling and replenishing your mind with things you've already learned. It's an ongoing process and is initiated by two critical sources: God's written Word and what the Holy Spirit speaks to you personally.

God wants you to replace what the world has programmed you to think with the paradigm of life that the Word of God gives you. That process is called renewal. Renewal is the process of adopting an entire system of values, an entire way of looking at life from the Bible's perspective that flows in an opposite direction from the world's system of thinking and living.

God wants you to study, understand, and adopt His way of thinking and use it to replace what the world has taught you during your years on earth.

What to Renew Your Mind to First

The foundation upon which the entire renewal process is built is found in the words of Jesus in John chapter 15:

If you abide in Me, and My words abide in you, you will ask what you desire, and it shall be done for you (NKJV).

The word *abide* has broad application, yet it certainly involves a reference to what we do with our minds as the statement "My words abiding in you" indicates. Yet this passage also reveals foundationally what we must renew our minds to. "If you abide in me" comes first in this passage, thus abiding involves being consciously aware of the indwelling presence of God in your life.

This is the foundation for renewing your mind properly. You must abide in Him which involves continually refilling and replenishing your conscious awareness of the presence of God in your life. Until you master this first step, your ability to have His words remain in you and impact your life in a positive way will be hindered. In fact, you could memorize the whole Bible and still not be transformed!

To experience transformation, you must become grounded (mentally renewed) in the fact that He never leaves you nor forsakes you. He's closer than your skin. He (the greater One) lives on the inside of you. You are the temple of the Holy Spirit. He goes with you wherever you go. You must *abide* in Him more and more by increasing your awareness of His indwelling presence in your life.

AN EXAMPLE OF ABIDING

John G. Lake, a powerful minister who lived in the early decades of the 19th century, mastered abiding in God. He was consciously aware of God living on the inside of him to the point that after he dressed each day, he would look in the mirror and talk to God—because he knew, he believed God lived on the inside of him. It was that real to John G. Lake.

No, he didn't believe he was God. But he did know that God lived in him because he was a Christian. We aren't to elevate ourselves in importance above God. We're not in a place of equality to God in the sense that He is no longer our power source. But we are living temples of His presence and we are to reveal Him to the world. We are to reveal Jesus to the world around us as we are the "body" of Christ. And the key to living this way is having an awareness of the indwelling presence of Christ.

During a typical day, how often are you aware of the presence of God in your life? If you're like most people, not much. But the first key to renewing your mind is to constantly be aware of and walk in the reality of God's indwelling presence. The result will be positive transformation.

I remember an experience I had some years ago when someone sued our church. At the time, it was shocking and devastating to me mentally. I just couldn't get over that someone would actually do that to us. Because of that, I felt vulnerable mentally and emotionally—until I began to abide in the Lord.

As I took time to abide in the Lord, I became more and more aware of the greater One living on the inside of me. By the time I had to go give depositions and such, I was thoroughly rooted and grounded in the fact that God was with me, for me, in me, and went before me to make crooked places straight!

When the man's lawyer began drilling me, making accusations and innuendoes, I started smiling. I wasn't being disrespectful, but it had become so real to me who was living in me that I got tickled that this guy had no idea with whom he was dealing. He was dealing with the greater One who lived on the inside of me! He was dealing with God almighty! Not just Mac Hammond.

This powerful revelation *transformed* me in the situation and, ultimately, *transformed* the entire situation as not too far down the road, the case was dropped as the judge dismissed it as frivolous. Abiding in Him can do the same for you!

On a broader scale when your mind is renewed to the truth of God being right there with you, as close as your skin, it will affect what you do, where you go, and the way you behave. Ultimately, it will bring a supernatural boldness that wouldn't otherwise be in your life as you generate a conscious moment by moment deliberate daily awareness of the greater One living inside of you.

WRONG DESIRES CHANGED—RIGHT DESIRES FULFILLED!

John 15:7 in the Wuest Bible translation reveals another aspect of what will be transformed as you truly abide and begin the process of renewing your mind as the Bible describes:

If you maintain a living communion with Me and My words are at home in you, then I command you to ask, at once, something for yourself whatever your heart desires and it will become yours.

Isn't that awesome?

He's saying that as you renew your mind and begin to maintain a conscious awareness of God's abiding presence, it is the foundation for your desires to be right and generated by the Holy Spirit—and then, when you ask something, it will automatically be in line with that desire and it will be yours.

The bottom line is this: if you become consciously aware and focus your thought life on the abiding presence of God, wrong desires will be changed and right desires will be generated that are in line with His will. And that makes it possible for God to say to you, "Ask. Do it now. Whatever things your heart desires, I can bring it to pass now."

That's how you live in the will of God for your life.

ABIDING = DELIGHTING

Doesn't this bring Psalm 37:4 into perspective?

Delight yourself also in the Lord and He shall give you the desires of your heart (NKJV).

Delighting yourself involves both abiding and using your mind. Delight is thinking. It's mentally imaging. It's meditating. It's getting your life in alignment with the Word. It's changing the way you see things. When you delight yourself, you abide in Him and thus you begin to analyze and evaluate every obstacle or decision you face in light of the fact that He is always with you and never leaves you.

That means when you get a bad report from the doctor, instead of thinking, *Oh, I'm going to die,* you think, *The Healer lives in me.*

That means when you hear the Holy Spirit tell you where to live, whom to marry, and so on, you'll recognize His voice. It won't be hard to figure out the will of God for your life and you'll know that's the way you're to go. Your delight will be His delight, because you abide in Him.

Once you are abiding in and constantly aware of the presence of God, you can tackle the things you need and want to change about your life. You can appropriately apply the promises of God to specific areas of your life and actually move deeper into renewing your mind to the truth God has for your life. Psalm 1:1-2 says:

Blessed is the man that walketh not in the counsel of the ungodly, nor standeth in the way of sinners, nor sitteth in the seat of the scornful. But his delight is in the law of the Lord; and in his law doth he meditate day and night.

The Psalm 1 man has separated himself unto the Lord and he has done it by delighting himself in the law of the Lord, which is the written Word of God. By delighting himself in the Word, he has built an image of his life in line with what God has spoken about him, and that's why he doesn't sit in the seat of the scornful, or stand in the way of the sinner, or walk in the counsel of the ungodly. Instead, he is like a tree planted by rivers of living water who brings forth fruit in due season, who prospers in all he does (verse 3). He has built an image of his life being lived in line with what God says about it.

Paint the Picture

I encourage you to cultivate looking at life through God's lens. Allow the Word of God to paint a picture on the canvas of your mind of God's plans and purposes for you. Remember, this is a continual process for renew that means: replenish, refill, refresh. The only way to live replenished, refilled, and refreshed is to be ever conscious of His abiding presence, His Word, and the specific insights He has spoken to you by the Holy Spirit.

Abide in Him by always focusing on Him. Let His words abide in you by delighting in His written Word and what the Holy Spirit says to you. Consistently imagine living in line with the picture this process paints. As you do, also begin to wean your mind from any patterns of thinking that do not contribute to the painting and you will start making significant progress towards God's high calling for you.

Weaning Your Mind

{Chapter 4}

The ideal way we are to live and interact with God is based on maturing to a place of trusting Him. That means we are patiently and consistently saying what we ought to be saying and doing what we ought to be doing—thus consistently expecting Him to perform His will in our lives. We are daily abiding in Him!

But the only way to truly live like this—and to trust Him in every way—is to not only renew our minds, but also wean them of detrimental thought patterns!

The level of trust God expects us to walk in is like that of a weaned child. Psalm 131:1-3 says:

Lord, my heart is not haughty, nor my eyes lofty; neither do I exercise myself in matters too great or in things too wonderful for me. Surely I have calmed and quieted my soul; like a weaned child with his mother, like a weaned child is my soul within me [ceased from fretting]. O Israel, hope in the Lord from this time forth and forever" (AMP).

The word *hope* in verse 3 literally means "trust." The most important aspect of our relationship with God is trust. It's even more important than faith, because you have to know the will of God to have faith. You have to know it before you can believe it. But trust is the only thing we have when we don't know the will of God.

In Psalm 37:5, the Lord says to commit your way unto Him. Why? Because it's the only way He can perform His will in your life—when you trust Him.

To truly trust the Lord and to be patient and expectant of His will manifesting in our lives requires that we be "weaned in our soul," just like a child is weaned from his mother.

The analogy of a weaned child in Psalm 131 communicates so much to us. When an infant is born, it is completely dependent on its mother for all sustenance, for life itself. When the Bible was written, this was more real than today. In biblical times, there was no infant formula of any kind. A mother nursed her baby to keep it alive and well. Her well-being determined the baby's well-being. There were no other options.

Then, there came a day when to continue the well-being of that child—to continue its normal growth and development—he/she needed to be weaned.

So the picture God is painting for us regarding our minds is this. There are things your mind is dependent on for life, things your mind is dependent on to be happy. There are things your mind says have to be in place for you to feel content or fulfilled. Your mind says your husband or wife must behave in a certain way, and treat you a certain way, or you can't possibly be content in this life. Your mind says all of that—until you wean it.

Oftentimes, your mind tells you that until you have more money, you can't be happy. Or if you could just get a new car, then you'd be happy. Or if you had new clothes, or nicer clothes, then you could be happy.

Single people's minds may tell them they can't be happy or complete until they find a mate. Their minds may have convinced them of that. Their self-images could be wrapped up in whether or not they marry. Their happiness could be dependent on finding that one special person.

All of these scenarios are being controlled and fed by minds that aren't weaned. Like a child who is dependent on suckling at his mother's breast, you are utterly dependent on particular circumstances in order to be content, satisfied, or happy.

So weaning the mind, in a general sense, is weaning yourself away from those ingrained dependencies that you think have to be there for you to be happy. It's recognizing and removing thought patterns, rationalities, or reasoning which produces mental agitation.

Yes, God made you a rational being, capable of reasoning through problems and decisions. He gave you the mental ability to think—to take information, assimilate it, and then arrive at the correct conclusion. In fact, He didn't create your mind to derive wrong conclusions. If you have enough correct and applicable information, you can always arrive at a valid conclusion because that's the way God made your mind. This God-given logical capacity is one of the many aspects that distinguishes you from any other life form.

God wants to give you the information you need to make good decisions. He wants to give you spiritual input about matters the Bible doesn't mention—like what occupation you're to have or where you are to live. That's why you need to spend time in His presence, learning to recognize His voice. That's why you need to know the written Word as well as how to hear Him.

Of course, God wants you to gather natural information also as you need a balance of both to make valid decisions. But we must be careful to not err on the side of carnal reasoning, which means using more natural data than spiritual data to make decisions. The fact is when you predominantly use carnal reasoning, you come to invalid conclusions! Thus your mind has to be weaned in order to eliminate all major agitations that can adversely affect your ability to make right and clear decisions.

Six Areas in Which We All Need Weaning

Psalm 131:2 says, "Like a weaned child is my soul within me [ceased from fretting]." To be weaned, you have to cease from fretting. In other words, if you're fretting about something, then you need to be weaned from it. Fretting means you're agitated, in inner turmoil, upset, uptight, bothered. It's any mental activity that produces agitation.

I've compiled a list of six ways people fret that I believe are the most prevalent in our lives. As I go through them, examine yourself and identify any ways you need to wean your mind.

Number One:
Resist Always Having to Have a Conclusion

Sometimes God doesn't give you enough information to arrive at a conclusion. Because of the way our minds are constructed, we always want a conclusion. Therefore, one of our common pitfalls is that if God doesn't give us enough information to arrive at a conclusion, we provide our own conclusions. The result is that we decide upon and believe wrong conclusions.

For example, (Problem) "Well, I've been up there three times and had hands laid on me, and I'm still not healed."

(Invalid conclusion) "God must not want me healed. It's not the will of God to heal everyone."

Do you see the faultiness of providing your own conclusion when you don't have enough information?

If God doesn't give you enough information—if the Holy Spirit doesn't speak to you and show you something—then you need to stop right there in your mind. You can't ask, "Why?" If you try to satisfy the "Why?" then you'll supply the rest of the data, and you'll be wrong. You'll arrive at faulty conclusions like, "It must not be God's will to heal me."

So when there isn't enough spiritual data for the rational process to lead you to a conclusion, the first sign of a mind that has been weaned is that it stops right there. A weaned mind doesn't have to know, "Why?" It doesn't have to know "When?"

Asking "Why?" produces agitation, and then an un-weaned mind will start supplying the answers—wrong answers!—that lead to wrong conclusions.

God has told us not to lean to our own understanding (Proverbs 3:5). He's told us that we see through a glass darkly for now (1 Corinthians 13:12).

God simply isn't going to give us all the answers today for every decision we will make between now and the rest of our lives. He will give us the information we need to make decisions for today. So learn to not give into your mind's demand to bring everything to a conclusion.

Number Two:
Rid Yourself of Defeatist Thinking

If you never quit, you win. That's how God thinks and that's how He wants you to think. God didn't make you a loser. He has never created losers. But people become losers for a lot of reasons, the first of which is they let a losing mentality begin growing in their lives. Having a defeatist or losing mentality will produce a lot of agitation and inner turmoil. If you don't think you will ever get promoted, if you're always worried about whether you will have enough money to put bread on the table, you will lose. If you worry that you won't make it in a new business venture, or if you always see the glass as half empty rather than half full, you won't make it.

Defeatist thinking is not of God. Wean yourself from that. Wean yourself from negative, defeatist thinking. Carnal reasoning will tell you, "You have to measure the odds here." Yes, you have to make informed decisions, but that doesn't mean your thoughts have to be dominated by failure or defeat.

God says in His Word that you are more than a conqueror through Him who loves you (Romans 8:37). You can do all things through Christ who strengthens you (Philippians 4:13). Believe what God says and not what negative thinking says.

Number Three:
Get Your Mind Off Self-Centered Thinking

In Philippians 2:4 it reads, "Look not every man on his own things, but every man also on the things of others." In other words, don't just think about your own stuff and your own needs. Think of others. Be concerned about the things of others. Be concerned about someone else's welfare.

It's natural for your mind to think about you. It wants to think about what you will eat today, where you will go, how you will entertain yourself, and on and on it goes. It will all be inward thinking unless you wean yourself from that way of thinking.

Number Four:
Wean Yourself of Self-Pity

Self-pity is similar to self-centered thinking, but it goes a step further. Self-pity is when you feel sorry for yourself. It's when you think, *Look how bad it is. I can't do anything about this. I'm hemmed in and it's not fair! It's not fair how they affect my life.*

When you begin to think about how bad things are for you, it only leads down one path—the path to depression. And depression leads to despair. And despair leads to death.

Never allow self-pity to go unchecked in your life. It's too dangerous. Reel it in and discipline yourself to obey the Word of God. Give thanks in all things (1 Thessalonians 5:18). Rejoice in the Lord always (Philippians 4:4). Weaning your mind off indulging in self-pity is a vital part of growing up spiritually and critical to controlling your soul.

Number Five:
Wean Yourself of Prideful Thoughts

Despite all the accolades of men and the achievements you've racked up in life, the truth remains, you've done nothing and accomplished nothing in your life except by the grace of God. When I first came back to God and started going to church again, I had a hard time with this concept. But it's still true. Even though I had become a very successful businessman and had made a lot of money, I really hadn't done it except by the grace of God. So to be prideful and boastful about it was sin.

We all have to come to grips with this.

"You mean I can't take credit for anything?"

No, you can't. John 15:5 tells us that without Christ, we can do nothing. Absolutely nothing.

Our human tendency is to think more highly of ourselves than we ought, but the Word of God cautions us against such thinking. So wean yourself of prideful thinking. You are what you are and you've become what you've become by the grace of God.

Number Six:
Stop Judgmental Thinking

Mankind has a strong tendency to point a finger and say, "Did you see that? Did you see what they did? Do you know what they did?" Judging others and telling all about it is a bad habit. Somehow it makes us feel less bad about all the habits we need to deal with in our own lives. Somehow we feel better, and we think it makes us look better when we put someone else down.

But all it really does is produce agitation.

And the agitation produces fretting. When you sow a judgmental approach to people, you're condemning. You're heaping guilt and condemnation on them—and that is what you will reap. And you will become one fretful person.

LET THE WEANING BEGIN!

All six of these patterns of thought produce fretting which is your number-one indicator that you haven't weaned your mind. In fact, anything that produces fretfulness in your heart, or agitation, or inner turmoil has to be weaned from your thinking. Only then can you completely renew your mind to a new way of thinking.

Don't give in to your mind's agitations. If you yield to your agitations, you will empower your mind to convince you that anything is the will of God. It literally has the capacity to do that.

Instead, wean your mind. Train it. And yield to the balance of information coming in from your spirit. What hangs in the balance is your position of trust, of patient expectation that enables God to meet your need. What hangs in the balance is the control of your soul and thus your destiny.

Yes, wrong thoughts which need to be weaned will come, yet don't feel bad when they do. Instead don't take those thoughts, don't speak those thoughts, don't dwell on them. Cast them down and focus on the picture of you fulfilling the will of God that is being painted on the canvas of your mind as you abide in Him and renew your mind with the Word of God!

Vain Imaginations

Hopefully by now you have begun to recognize wrong behavior comes from wrong thinking and is the product of an imagination which has not been renewed or weaned. The fact is when behavior deviates from the way God intends and mandates in His Word, it is a byproduct of what the Bible calls vain imaginations.

We have defined the word *vain* in an earlier chapter this way: empty, worthless, or with no purpose. What I want you to see is that anything you don't find in the Bible or doesn't originate and align with the God's principles is *vain*. This makes some people mad to hear but it's a fact. Everything that really works in this life does so because it is a God idea. In other words, vain imaginations build a picture of our lives on the basis of anything other than a God idea found in God's Word.

In Romans 8:6, the Bible calls it being *carnally minded* and reveals the result—death! Of course, death is not always instantaneous; it usually is a process of corruption that takes you steadily downhill. It's often slow and sometimes hard to see. But death is the ultimate result of being carnally minded or allowing vain imaginations to dominate our thinking. So our ability to eliminate vain imaginations and properly focus our thought life is a critical aspect of soul control.

Second Corinthians 10:3 says, "For though we walk in the flesh, we do not war after the flesh [verse 4 is parenthetical] for the weapons of our warfare are not carnal [that means temporal or natural] but mighty through God to the pulling down of strong holds." And then verse 5 describes our warfare; "Casting down imaginations, and every high thing that exalteth itself against the knowledge of God, and bringing into captivity every thought to the obedience of Christ." The war for control of your soul is described here and the battleground is the mind where there are three levels of mental activity: thoughts, imaginations, and strongholds.

Thoughts are going to come from every direction, sometimes at a dizzying rate. They are generated by every word that's spoken to you, things that you see, and every circumstance you encounter. It's not possible or practical to seek to categorize all of your thoughts, for the normal course of life is going to produce thousands of them each day. Yet, obviously, not all thoughts are good thoughts, so you must learn to select the thoughts that you're going to dwell upon and cast down other thoughts if you are going to control your soul.

In Matthew 6:25, Jesus said to *take no thought* about what you're going to eat, or what you're going to wear, or where you're going to live. By this we can clearly see you've got a choice of which thoughts you're going to dwell upon. In other words, you must be sure you don't *take* as yours every thought that comes to you.

Thoughts are the first level of mental activity discussed; the next are imaginations as we have discussed in other chapters. When you begin to ponder, meditate, and think about a thought, you isolate it in the realm of your mind and begin building a mental image in your imagination which will eventually produce behavior. Thus thoughts are the root of the matter; essentially, you're building a scenario for a piece of your life around a thought that you've taken.

STRONGHOLDS DEFINED

Imaginations become strongholds when the behavior produced becomes consistent and contrary to your best interests. Bad habits, addictive, or compulsive behavior is indicative of the presence of a stronghold in your mind. And because of the wording in this passage regarding warfare and stronghold, we know these are wrong thoughts that have produced wrong behavior. Also, since a stronghold is defined as enemy fortification, we can assume the kingdom of darkness is involved.

Satan and his demonic host can't read your mind. Yet they can observe your life and listen to your words. And when that realm of darkness observes deviant behavior or hears words which reveal vain imaginations, it will make an effort to bring this arena of your thought life to the level of a stronghold by manipulating circumstance and unwitting people to cause you to have repeated opportunity to continue in the wrong behavior.

For example, I've never demonstrated a weakness for drugs and I've never had a pusher try to sell me drugs. But isn't it funny, somebody coming off drugs has dozens of opportunities to buy or to use again. You think that's coincidence? Absolutely not!

Yes, God has created us to become creatures of habit which is not inherently wrong. Yet it is important to understand the kingdom of darkness can distort that by promoting and enabling bad behavior. So when it comes to casting down thoughts and dealing with vain imaginations, the first arena you have to deal with is strongholds.

The good news is the Bible says the weapons of our warfare are not carnal but mighty through God. When a wrong imagi-nation has progressed to a point where it's become a stronghold, the anointing of God can be brought to bear to destroy that yoke of bondage.

The anointing, or manifest presence of the Holy Spirit, is administered in a lot of ways. It can be by the laying on of hands. It is often manifest in times of praise and worship with the glory of God being present in the sanctuary. It also can simply be a product of the operation of the gifts of the Spirit which nobody controls; it is as the Spirit wills. But when strongholds are present, the anointing of God needs to be applied so you have the latitude to begin controlling your own imagination.

DEALING WITH VAIN IMAGINATIONS

Let's look into the primary cause of vain imaginations. In Romans 1:20-21 it says:

For the invisible things of him from the creation of the world are clearly seen, being understood by the things that are made, even his eternal power and Godhead; so that they are without excuse: Because that, when they knew God, they glorified him not as God, neither were thankful; but became vain in their imaginations, and their foolish heart was darkened.

Through wrong thinking and vain imaginations, these people began to mentally image their lives unfolding in a way that was not consistent with God's Word but rather with what the world said. They were using the law of the mind wrongly and open to vain imaginations because they were not giving God glory by being thankful to Him.

This almost seems too simplistic yet it reveals a great deal about the power of praise and worship—a time set aside specifically to give God glory and thank Him for what He has done. Many people participate in the teaching or preaching parts of a typical service, but don't get into the music. This is especially true with men or those who cannot sing very well. What they fail to recognize is that they are missing out on one of the most powerful opportunities to cast down vain imaginations, control their souls, and fulfill their destinies.

Of course, you need to be thankful and give God glory more than just on Sunday, but begin to seize the moment as a time to exercise proper control of your soul. When you do, your imagination is supernaturally freed to build a picture of your life on the basis of what God says about you. In other words, you won't be as subject or as open to vain imaginations and you will minimize the impact of what the world says.

Giving Thanks Well

In 1 Corinthians 14:17, the apostle Paul reveals another great way to be thankful and thus deal with the potential for vain imaginations. It says; "For thou verily givest thanks well…" and in context, it is clearly talking about praying in the Spirit in other tongues. For he says in verse 14, "If I pray in an unknown tongue, my spirit prayeth, but my understanding is unfruitful."

I know in my life there have been times when I really want to give thanks to God but it just seemed hollow to say "Thank You, Lord." It didn't express adequately what was in my heart. When I expressed my heart through praying and worshipping in the Spirit, the impact was immediate.

Here is the point I want to make. If your thinking has been confused and it's produced any level of mental torment, oppression, or depression, one of the primary remedies is being thankful and giving God glory. One powerful way to do this is to spend time praying and worshipping *in the Spirit.* This will not only help eradicate vain imaginations, it will also keep you connected to the anointing of God and make you more responsive to His Word.

Thought Selection

When strongholds are dealt with and thankfulness is in place, thought selection becomes the most basic daily task for avoiding and dealing with vain imaginations. And the thought selection process has everything to do with what you say. We can look back to Matthew chapter 6 where Jesus talked quite a bit about *taking no thought*. He tells us how the process occurs in verse 31, "Therefore take no thought *saying…*" You don't really take a thought and begin to build an imagination with it until you put words to it. So the way we begin to cast down thoughts and exercise our imagination in the way God intends is by putting the Word of God in our mouths.

The story of Joshua is enlightening in this arena. Joshua was preparing to lead the children of Israel into the Promised Land, a land that flows with milk and honey. It was also a land that Joshua knew well as he was one of those sent in to spy out the land. He knew well and had seen for himself the many formidable obstacles they faced in occupying the land. I am sure there were many *thoughts* flooding Joshua's mind as the children of Israel gazed across the Jordan river and in the valley saw the walled city of Jericho.

God said I've given you the land but here's what you've got to do to take it. First of all in Joshua 1:8 he says, "This book of the law shall not depart out of your mouth." Well, of course, Joshua has to know what God said for faith to arise in his heart as faith comes by hearing (and hearing) the Word of God. That's the principle reason you put the Word in your mouth, so you can hear it and faith will come.

Now it's important that your behavior corresponds with your faith, so the second thing God told Joshua is to *meditate therein day and night*. In other words, Joshua was to be sure that the thoughts that filled his mind were consistent with the plans and purposes of God. Joshua needed to not allow any vain imaginations to develop based on all the natural information he had about the land. Instead he needed to imagine winning the battle of Jericho, imagine overcoming all of the obstacles that were set before him, and imagine partaking of a land that flows with milk and honey.

God told Joshua to keep speaking the Word and meditate on it day and night. Which means to ponder it, turn it over in your mind, focus your thoughts upon it, consider it, build a scenario for your life on the basis of that Word. The result will be you'll observe to do according to that Word and thus will prosper and have good success.

As we have said, the law of the mind is always at work, thus the negative working of this process is often very subtle. Often somebody will ask you a question that provides a vehicle for you to put words to a wrong thought. You could be having trouble in a particular relationship and someone will innocently ask you how it is going. Be careful of the *thoughts* you take as yours when you answer! Your words begin building an imagination which will either reinforce the problem or promote a positive solution.

Why do you think God told Joshua "Don't let the Word depart out of your mouth," and then meditate on it day and night. Because by putting the Word of God in his mouth, he was *taking* God's thoughts. This reveals the process for using our imagination properly is to select the thoughts we take and the thoughts that we don't take with the words of our mouths. When you speak the Word of God and meditate on God's thoughts, you're casting down vain imaginations. You are building a platform for your behavior to align with God's purposes. You are on your way to controlling your soul as God intends!

THE SOUL

{section 1}

[emotions]   [will]   [mind]

I feel.

Why Your
Feelings Matter

God created you with the capacity to feel. He created you to have emotions, and He has a purpose for your emotions. Though religion has told us that our emotions are bad, or not important, God created your emotions to be the strongest motivator of your consistent behavior. No, you aren't to make decisions based entirely on your emotions, but God does intend for your emotions to support the thinking of your renewed mind so that you have sufficient motivation not to waver in your decision making. The bottom line is that emotions are necessary to the decision-making process.

James writes that a wavering man, or a double-minded man, receives nothing from the Lord (James 1:6). Wavering is not of God. Going back and forth is not of God. So your staying power, your source of consistency and persistency, is rooted in your understanding of how to control and direct the emotional part of your being.

People who are thinking about quitting smoking are a good example of what I'm talking about. Now, it doesn't take a lot of intellectual activity to arrive at the conclusion that smoking is killing them. They know that. They know it's rotting out their lungs, they can't breathe as well as a nonsmoker, and that their life expectancy is greatly diminished.

So it doesn't take a lot of information to convince people that smoking is detrimental to their health, and that knowledge initiates the desire in them to want to quit. But if their minds are the only part of their souls engaged in deciding to quit smoking, they might quit for a day or two, if that long, and they'll be right back at it.

Why? Because for them to succeed and stay motivated, the emotional part of their souls have to be actively engaged as well.

If people really want to quit smoking, they have to have some fire in their eyes about it. They've got to be stirred up about it. They've got to get righteously indignant about this enemy which has brought this horrible dependency into their lives. They've got to get angry about it. They've got to get fired up, so they'll have the staying power to see their decisions through to the desired end.

This is how God intended for your emotional being to function.

Yes, we tend to categorize some emotions as bad—expressions like fear, anger, hatred, resentment, jealousy, and sorrow, for example. But if God made us capable of these emotions, He must have some divine purpose for depositing them within us. And He does. It's not accurate to categorize emotions as bad or good. They are all necessary when used in the right way.

God wants you to learn how to direct all your emotional capacities properly, and to cultivate them in a way that will give you the kind of staying power necessary once you make decisions. He wants you to learn how to use all the emotions He gave you in a positive way. It's only when they're out of control or directed wrongly that they become bad instead of good.

In the next chapter, I will examine different kinds of emotion and how we're to cultivate them and intensify them. But for now, I want to teach you how uncontrolled emotions can have a disastrous effect in three main areas of your life. Emotions are good. They are God-given. But left uncontrolled, they are devastating to your experience of life.

UNCONTROLLED EMOTIONS KILL YOUR FAITH

Faith comes by hearing. The Bible tells us that. It comes by hearing and hearing and hearing. It's an ongoing process. To stay in faith, you have to keep hearing the truth. Therefore, if you come to a place of faith where you truly believe something will come to pass, if your emotions are uncontrolled, they will sabotage your faith.

In other words, if you come to a place of believing, unless you act on that belief, it will never produce fruit in your life. We have discussed what causes behavior, but what is the most powerful motivator of human behavior? It is what you *feel*. The strongest feelings you have will be reflected in your most consistent behavior. If you are not controlling your emotions properly to undergird what you've decided to believe, then your behavior will be inconsistent.

I'll give you a good example from my own life. I believe that love never fails (1 Corinthians 13:8). I believe that with all my heart. I believe it because I've heard enough Word over the years to know that I know love never fails. Never! I've seen it work in my life and in the lives of others to absolutely transform them and situations. But even so, I've had plenty of occasions in my life for someone to stir me up and for my emotions to start churning. I've felt the anger rise, and even though I believe love never fails, my uncontrolled emotion has killed my corresponding action for what I believe. Therefore, in this area of my life, my faith was killed. Love didn't manifest. Anger did.

Uncontrolled emotions will kill your faith.

UNCONTROLLED EMOTIONS CORRUPT DECISION MAKING

Your emotional component is designed to support or undergird decisions you make. It is not intended to be the basis for decisions. Feelings are never to be the basis for any decisions. God didn't design you to make decisions based on the way you feel. You aren't to do something or not do it based on feelings. You are not to call in sick just because you didn't feel like going to work. You are not to skip school just because you didn't feel like going.

But isn't this way of living prevalent in our modern society? Yet, it is not how God created mankind to function.

Consider godly emotions like being generous or thoughtful. You will never feel like being generous or thoughtful. Those are attributes that you must learn to control, channel, and properly cultivate because your natural flesh will never lead you that way. You have to avoid making decisions on the basis of feelings.

I heard once about how the military trains dogs for use in the field. The first step in training is to teach the dog to fetch, which is almost an instinctive response. Once a dog is well developed in fetching and retrieving, the handler will throw the item to be fetched, but he will command the dog to stay.

If the dog stays even though his every muscle may be twitching, his ears flicking, his tail wagging, then he is fit for further training and use in battle.

But if that dog doesn't stay, he doesn't pass the test for use in battle.

Why? Because his emotions are uncontrolled, and he'll be a danger instead of an asset on the field.

How do you react when God tells you something? How do you respond when He tells you to stay, or wait, or slow down?

Excitement is good. Anticipation is good. But uncontrolled, they become detrimental.

Before we built our new church building, I knew every inch of it in my heart. I had seen it in my heart. I knew it was ours. It was something we had to have. I was like that dog wanting to go fetch so badly I couldn't stand it.

But I had to wait. I had to wait on the timing of the Lord and the financing. I didn't want to stay in the old building. It was filled with problems because we had grown so large. It was filled with traffic problems and overcrowding. Two banks and a third financial institution were willing to work with us. The pressure to run from it was immense.

But God said, "Stay."

That was hard. I didn't feel like staying. But, thank God, I did. Today we are blessed with an awesome sanctuary all because we kept our emotions in control. We didn't make decisions based on how we felt.

"But, Mac, I feel like the Lord wants me to do thus and so."

Just because you *feel* something or you *don't feel* something doesn't mean that's what you should or shouldn't do. God says in His Word that He'll confirm His Word to you in the mouth of two or three witnesses. Hang around a little longer. Give God time to confirm His ways to you. Let Him prove to you that you're on the right track.

UNCONTROLLED EMOTIONS CAUSE YOU TO JUDGE WRONGLY

When your emotions are left uncontrolled, one of the directions they'll take is to judge other people—to become judgmental. We discussed weaning your mind from this tendency and the reason God doesn't want you judging others is because 90 percent of the time, blessing comes into your life through others. If you judge someone, then you have just cut them off from possibly blessing you and from you being able to be a blessing to them.

I experienced this firsthand one time with a young man who had been coming to our church for about one year. Without realizing it, I had judged him to be a flake. He dressed funny, talked funny, and acted funny compared to what I was used to. He said a few strange things to me here and there, so without really consciously doing it, I judged him.

One Sunday, he came up to me and said he had a word to tell me. Because I had subconsciously judged him as a flake, I listened and was polite, but I didn't expect him to be a reliable or credible source.

Boy, was I wrong! His word was a confirming word. It was right on target about something the Lord had been dealing with me about. Because of my judgment, I had cut off that channel of blessing, and I realized it had cost me about two months of time and some pain.

I learned the lesson, and I'm passing it on to you. Don't let uncontrolled emotion cause you to judge others.

MAINTAINING YOUR EMOTIONS IS MAINTAINING YOUR SUCCESS

God wants you to learn how to direct and control your emotional responses. They are the key to your maintaining the momentum that can carry you to success.

Think about your giving for a moment. Think about the things you are believing for in your life, in your marriage, career, or family. What part do your emotions play in bringing those things into manifestation?

Galatians 6:7 says:

Be not deceived; God is not mocked: for whatsoever a man soweth, that shall he also reap. For he that soweth to his flesh shall of the flesh reap corruption; but he that soweth to the Spirit shall of the Spirit reap life everlasting. And let us not be weary in well doing: for in due season we shall reap, if we faint not.

How do you *faint not*? How do you hang in there until there is a manifestation? How do you not grow weary and discouraged? You do it by keeping your emotions in control.

You have to become emotionally involved in the decisions you make in order to cultivate the kinds of feelings that eliminate the possibility of weariness and fainting. Otherwise, you'll never make it through your due season to your harvest.

You need your emotions behind the decisions you've made so you'll be motivated to keep sowing good seed during the hard times—to keep believing during the hard times and to hang in there until harvest.

So how do you cultivate your feelings properly?

Remember Romans 12:2, "And be not conformed to this world: but be ye transformed by the renewing of your mind, that ye may prove what is that good, and acceptable, and perfect, will of God."

Yes, this verse is about renewing your mind, but the things you think about the most are what you feel the strongest about. Feelings are generated by thoughts. Even though Romans 12:2 doesn't talk about emotions directly, we know that you can't get to the perfect will of God, and you can't experience the transformation with uncontrolled emotions.

The truth is you haven't renewed your mind until you've changed your feelings! If you still feel differently than the renewed mind suggests you should feel, then you haven't really renewed your mind. So the process of renewing your mind in some area isn't complete until your feelings have changed.

Your feelings have to support your thought process in order for you to reach success.

God wants you to feel what you've decided.

He wants you to feel He's right there beside you. He wants you to feel you are more than a conqueror through Him who loves you. He wants you to feel there's nothing the enemy can do to keep you from realizing the plan of God for your life. He wants you to feel an absolute confidence and trust in His goodness and faithfulness to you. He wants you to feel He will never leave you nor forsake you.

Your feelings matter.

Minimizing the Wrong Emotions—Fear and Anger

{Chapter 7}

What you think about the most is what you feel strongest about. I've told you that several times now, but I want it to become real to you. If you feel stronger about your hobby than you do your job, then you'll spend more time reflecting on your hobby, meditating on your hobby, and thinking about your hobby.

Therefore, the way you direct and intensify your emotions in a particular direction is by filling your mind with what the Word of God says about that particular emotion.

As a culture, we tend to lump our emotions into one of two categories: either positive emotions or negative emotions. But the truth is, God has given us the capacity to feel a wide range of emotions, so there must be a way to properly direct those feelings in order to realize the will of God for our lives.

That's not to say that everything you feel is of God. Satan—the enemy of your soul—does labor to pervert your feelings. For example, according to the Word of God, the love of God is shed abroad in our hearts (Romans 5:5). How? It is shed abroad in our hearts by the Holy Spirit. So, we have the capacity to love. Since Satan can't stop that, or trump it, or produce a counterfeit to it, he seeks to corrupt it. He seeks to turn it into lust, something to be consumed on self.

Fear is another example. We are to fear the Lord, to give Him reverence, honor, and respect. We are to be in awe of Him.

It's an emotional capacity that motivates us and propels us in our pursuit of God. But the enemy corrupts that fear into being something we wrestle with concerning our finances, well-being, or families—something God never intended. Satan endeavors to pervert our capacity to feel the fear of the Lord, something not rooted in a fear for our own well-being.

All of our feelings that are God given, Satan seeks to corrupt and turn our focus inward toward self.

To help you see how this happens over and over in so many of our emotions, I want to show you four foundational capacities in which I believe most emotion is rooted. I'll show you two in this chapter and two in the next chapter. By understanding these four foundational capacities, you can better understand the myriad of emotions you experience, as well as those the people around you experience. By learning how to manage these four basic emotional response patterns from which all other feelings are related, you can learn how to better control and direct them, thus having a handle on a broad range of feelings.

Because we like to categorize emotions as negative or positive, let's look at our capacities in this light. On the negative end of the spectrum is fear. Tied closely to fear is anger, because most anger is rooted in fear. On the positive end of the spectrum is love—not *agape* love, but *phileo* love, which is the capacity to feel love or affection. Ongoing love and affection are motivated by compassion.

So on one end we have fear and anger, and on the other end is love and compassion. Those are what I believe are the four foundational capacities of emotion, from which all other related feelings and emotions stem. As I teach you concerning each one, get glimpses of how you can better manage and control your emotions so they aren't controlling you.

THE BATTLE FOR YOUR SOUL

Anger is a favorite tool of the enemy, and it is one of the most corrosive feelings or emotional responses one person gives another that ruins relationships—relationships God intends to use to bring blessing to your life. In other words, 90 percent of God's blessings or direct ministry into your life comes through other people. Very seldom does God appear in a puffy white cloud or drop a bag of coins on your head. No. He uses people to bring ministry or blessing to you and then through you. Therefore, the single most often used ploy of Satan is to generate anger toward people!

Think of a marriage. This is probably the greatest relationship challenge on earth because God has joined you with someone whom God intends to use in your life in a very unique way. Yet, marriage is the relationship where anger and the resulting schism often prevents God from ministering to one through the other. Hurtful words are said. Angry words are said. The walls are built. The husband and wife withdraw from each other, because neither wants to be hammered at again.

Effectively, Satan completely incapacitates the relationship from being able to be used by God. Satan knows that anger severs relationships, and it makes it impossible for God to minister through people He drew together.

Yes, anger is a godly capacity, but how we use it tends to be ungodly. We tend to misdirect it. All through the Word, we see examples of God hating, God getting angry, or God being jealous. We see emotions attributed to God that we normally would have written off as inappropriate or as bad emotional responses.

What God wants us to see and understand is that there is a righteous way to be angry or jealous. There is a way to be righteously indignant, even a way to hate correctly.

In fact, if you don't learn to cultivate your feelings properly, you will never be properly motivated or propelled down the path of God's will for your life.

For example, God does not hate the sinner. He hates the sin.

He loves the sinner. For God so loved the world, He gave His only begotten Son! (John 3:16) But He hates sin. He is intolerant, righteously indignant of the enemy's incursion into the lives of His children.

Therefore, we should be the same way. We should hate sin. We should hate evil. We should hate it so much that when we see it cropping up in our neighborhoods, we don't turn a blind eye to it. Rather, we become involved and motivated to begin allowing God to use us to deal with issues in our society.

Until we are truly righteously indignant at the encroachment of Satan and how he weasels his way into our lives, we'll never boot him out! We'll never get rid of the sin in our own lives until we hate sin like God does!

God is a jealous God, but not in the sense that a man is jealous of a woman and wants to consume all her charms on himself. God's righteous jealousy should manifest in us when we see someone backsliding. When we see them slipping back into the world, we should be jealous enough to go after them. We should get angry at the enemy.

But the only way you will—and most Christians will—is to first spend enough time renewing your mind to the truth of the battle that is being waged behind the scenes for your soul.

Virtually everything we deal with in life has a spiritual root. Ephesians 6:12 tells us that our anger and the way we relate to people is rooted in the fact we don't wrestle against flesh and blood, but against principalities and powers and rulers of darkness in high places. That needs to be very real to you.

Your problem is not your wife, your husband, your parents, your children, friends, boss, supervisor, or teacher. It's no one made of flesh and blood. Yet, the enemy of your soul labors to direct your indignation and anger toward people.

Satan knows that if he can direct your negative attention and emotion toward others, then he can cut off your relationship with the Lord. So he labors to focus your anger on other people.

Anger is defined as "an intense emotional state induced by displeasure." What is the source of your displeasure?

Very often, we become displeased with our lives because we perceive that God isn't answering our prayers. But all good things come from God (James 1:17), and all things that bring displeasure don't come from Him. They originate with the enemy of your soul.

Yes, Satan is a defeated foe. But he is still widely capable in terms of promoting his own agenda. He is a real opponent. He is intensely real in his quest to pull you away from the will of God for your life and to bring you displeasure.

When someone displeases you or you become displeased with a circumstance or a situation, it can produce anger. Remember, anger is an intense emotional response induced by displeasure. So when you become angry, remember where the displeasure that incited you originated—with the enemy of your soul.

When I was first born again, I had trouble internalizing this. I had no trouble believing in God, but it was hard for me to give Satan any credit for being a worthy opponent. In Christ, he's no match for me. But I have to apply all that I am in Christ to resist his influence.

The bottom line is that you are not in any contest with any person. You are not wrestling with people. You are wrestling with powers and principalities.

When people get under your skin, think about the warfare they're under. Think about the powers and principalities influencing them, and allow compassion to rise up and help you see them the way God does.

Seek to never direct anger toward another person, no matter how badly you want to put a name and a face to your anger. That's not what God created anger for. If you have a meeting scheduled with someone who has the tendency to incite you, prepare yourself spiritually and mentally ahead of time. Spend time with the Lord. Remind yourself that you're not dealing with flesh and blood. This is a spiritual matter. When all the related emotions of anger, hatred, bitterness, and resentment rise up, remember they all stem from unresolved anger, which is rooted in fear.

Direct your emotions in the way they should go. Direct your anger toward the dark forces that come against the plan of God in the earth. Hate sin. Resent what the enemy does to thwart the will of God in your life and others' lives.

Renew your mind to this truth every day. It's an ongoing journey all through life.

If you'll get angry with the right party, it will charge you down the path of God's will for your life like nothing else in this earth.

TIPS FOR CONTROLLING YOUR ANGER

James 1:19 says, "Wherefore, my beloved brethren, let every man be swift to hear, slow to speak, slow to wrath: For the wrath of man worketh not the righteousness of God."

Be slow to let anger enter your relationships or discussions. In other words, don't engage your tongue before you engage your brain. Then, be quick to listen. Repeat back to the person what you think they're saying, and if you're wrong, give them time to correct it. Give yourself time to stay cool and keep your tongue under control.

Since anger is rooted in fear, recognize that lots of people get angry because they feel intimidated or threatened. They become offended and that generates anger.

Perhaps you fall for this trap all too often. If you do, deal with the force of fear in your life. Second Timothy 1:7 says God has not given you a spirit of fear, but of power, love, and a sound mind. One of the best ways to deal a blow to fear in your life is to pray in tongues. That stirs up the power of God in your life. The Bible says when you pray in tongues, it edifies you. It builds you up. It pulls you out of this place of anxiety that takes you down a wrong path.

First John 4:18 says that perfect love casts out fear. So when you love someone, when you give to them (because that's what love does) it takes your focus off your own concerns. It turns your interest outward and defeats fear, because all fear is rooted in self-interest. Satan's perversion of your capacity to feel reverence for God (which is fear) is rooted in self-interest. So by loving people, you are turning your interests outward, thus moving away from fear.

Second Timothy said you have a sound mind. Keep it that way by bringing every thought captive to the obedience of Christ. Cast down vain imaginations and only think God's thoughts.

When you combine these three things—1) relying in faith on the indwelling presence of the Holy Spirit and the power He brings, 2) focusing your attention outward, 3) bringing your thoughts that produce anxiety or fear captive—then you will triumph over the enemy's perversion of fear in your life. You eliminate the root of much anger and its many associated feelings.

Lastly, I want you to see the result of what happens if you've already gotten angry and blown a relationship or two. Second Corinthians chapter 7 talks about grief and sorrow. It mentions there is a sorrow that leads to repentance and one that doesn't.

All too often, after you've blown something, grief and sorrow settle in. They are the result of anger, of unresolved issues, from a battle with someone. Think about it. If you engage in a serious disagreement with someone, you are left with a residue of heaviness. If you deal with it and repent, it leaves. But if you don't, it builds up over time. It becomes sadness and sorrow. It becomes discouragement and depression. It's oppressive. And it leads to death.

But godly sorrow is the sorrow that leads to repentance. It leads to something good and profitable. It leads you to growth. Second Corinthians 7:8 says:

For even though I did grieve you with my letter, I do not regret [it now], though I did regret it; for I see that that letter did pain you, though only for a little while (AMP).

The capacity to feel sorrow is of God if it lasts only a little while and leads you to repentance. God doesn't want or intend for people to be grieved all their lives. He doesn't want people oppressed or in despair much of their lives.

What God wants us to feel is a sorrow that leads to repentance, that contributes to salvation and deliverance from evil, and that never brings regret.

God's sorrow makes you realize you need to turn something around and do it differently. It takes you down a path of life and not death. It gets your attention to help you realize you've stepped off the path.

So all negative emotion is rooted in fear and anger, but once we redirect it to the way God intended, it helps produce the life we've always wanted!

Intensifying the Right Emotions—
Love and Compassion
{Chapter 8}

If you can get your anger, fear, and your resentment under control and focused in the right direction, then you can get all your other emotional responses under control—all through dealing with your anger and fear.

The same principle is true for the positive end of the emotional spectrum. If you can get the primary capacity of the positive emotions—love and compassion—focused in the right direction, you will find great peace in your life.

When you become a person perfected in love, as the Bible calls it, you will be living a life of peace. You will find great joy and feelings of happiness, fulfillment, and contentment. The truth is that all positive emotional responses are rooted in our capacity to love, because love never fails (1 Corinthians 13:8). Love is the only thing that can bring peace to any relationship. Love has the power to reduce the turmoil that often comes through other people. Love has the power to bring a tranquil condition in your family, as well as in every other area of your life. Love is what reaches out, gives, and brings joy.

I used to think that if I had a little more money, I would be happier. But the more money I made, the more miserable I became, because money has no capacity to produce joy. Having a different spouse, different job, being healed, having a new house—none of that has the capacity to bring joy.

Changes in circumstances generate a fleeting satisfaction, but joy on a long-term basis, true fulfillment, only comes to the human heart from loving and serving others.

It's such a hard lesson to learn, because everything in our flesh and everything in our society stimulates us to keep our eyes on ourselves.

EMOTIONAL LOVE DEFINED

The kind of love I'm referencing is *phileo.* In the Greek it means "brotherly love." The other Greek word for *love* in the New Testament is *agape.* The word "love" is used 160 times in the New Testament—*agape,* 143 times and *phileo,* 17 times.

Agape is expressed by giving to others, so obviously God is emphasizing our need to give even when we don't feel like it. But the *feeling* of affection—*phileo*—is crucially important in sustaining our decisions to *agape,* or give to other people.

The kind of love that never fails is the kind that looks to other people's needs and gives to meet their needs. It gives time, encouragement, help, or money. It's the kind that is consistent. It's what sums up all of Christianity. It is the highest law.

But to maintain a consistent life of loving, you will have to learn to cultivate feelings of affection and compassion.

It's really easy to understand. Who are the easiest people for you to give to? They are the ones you feel affection for, the ones you have compassion for. According to W.E. Vine's definition of *phileo,* the feeling of love is the response to the excellence of the object of affection. In other words, when you see someone who is excellent in virtue or character, it makes you feel good about them. When someone likes you or loves you, it makes you feel good about them.

But for the other 99 percent of the people in the world, you will have to draw on compassion to love them. They won't have the kind of character or virtue you find attractive. There must be something in you—love—to sustain you when you don't find someone attractive and when you don't feel affection for them.

STIRRING UP THE LOVE

Years ago, I couldn't feel any compassion for the lost. Intellectually, I knew I needed to preach the Gospel and reach the lost, but I didn't have "feelings" of compassion for them. It was hard on me mentally, because being a pastor, I was supposed to have that. But deep in my heart, I found it hard to have feelings for faceless masses of people.

But I changed. I changed by renewing my mind. I knew that without love, my faith would never work, and my ability to reach the lost depended on my ability to love them and be affectionate and compassionate toward them. First John 4:16-18 says:

We have known and believed the love that God hath to us. God is love; and he that dwelleth in love dwelleth in God, and God in him. Herein is our love made perfect, that we may have boldness in the day of judgment: because as he is, so are we in this world. There is no fear in love; but perfect love casteth out fear: because fear hath torment. He that feareth is not made perfect in love.

This verse is a perfect picture of fear being at one end of the spectrum and love being at the other. When the enemy is able to corrupt and steer the direction of your capacity to feel fear from the Lord to circumstance or man, the immediate antidote is the love of God.

Fear is always rooted in the big "I."

Love is always turned outward.

So if you become perfect in love, there is no room for fear. Perfect love casts out fear.

Fear has torment that takes on all kinds of forms—anxiety, worry, complaining, whining, pouting. Putting words to the fear in your life negatively affects your life. So resist the moaning and grumbling. Don't give it place in you. You need that love that casts out all fear.

Watch for the indicators of fear. If it is present in any form, get back over into love.

Then get your emotions lined up with your love walk. When your love is made perfect, your affections and feelings are lined up with your choice to walk in love, to give to others.

Notice verse 16: "We have known and believed the love that God hath to us. God is love; and he that dwelleth in love dwelleth in God, and God in him. Herein is our love made perfect…"

Herein where?

The previous verse has the answer. It's when you know and believe the love God has for you. That's where the power source is to loving others.

But how often do you spend time thinking about how much God loves you?

Before you focus on loving others, focus on how much God loves you. It will fuel your ability to love others with excellence.

Therein is your love made perfect.

YOU ARE THE APPLE OF HIS EYE

Everything that comes to you comes by choice. God has set before you life and blessing, and death and cursing. You have to choose which you will have. You have to choose what you will believe.

Then, once you've decided, your faith will only work by love—by your being perfected in love (Galatians 5:6).

When you are perfected in love, when you are truly aware of God's love for you, you won't ever have a hard time giving to others. It will do wonders for your faith when you are convinced you are the apple of God's eye. If He loves you as much as the Bible says He does, He is not going to withhold any good thing from you. The Bible says that if we as earthly parents know how to give good gifts to our children, how much more will God give to us! (Luke 11:13)

I know if you're a parent, it's normal to do anything to help your kids through life. Yes, you can get aggravated with them, but there's something in a parent that cannot let a kid experience difficulty that he can help him avoid. Most parents would go to the ends of the earth for their kids.

God is just like that! He feels more toward us than we can understand, just like a parent feels so much toward a child that the child never understands until he or she becomes a parent as well.

God is so in touch with you that He knows the number of hairs on your head! There's no reason for you to wander around from one day to the next not trusting God wondering if He will come through for you or not.

You are the apple of God's eye! He loves you. He hears your petitions. His thoughts are always toward you. John 17:23 says God loves you as much as He loves Jesus.

I remember being in Colorado a few years back on a hunting trip. I was on the side of a mountain at sunrise in the Rockies overlooking a meadow with a creek running through it. Just as the sun began to crack the edge of the ridge, I was overwhelmed with the sense that God made this little meadow and creek just for me. I was overwhelmed with how much God loves me.

I wasn't being arrogant. I was being filled with appreciation and gratefulness for His all-consuming love for me.

That's how we have to live each and every day. We have to renew our minds from thinking, *I'm not good enough to be loved.* Or, *I'm second best.*

No! God loves you as much as Jesus! He sent His only Son just for you! Romans 8:31 says:

What shall we then say to these things? If God be for us, who can be against us? He that spared not his own Son, but delivered him up for us all, how shall he not with him also freely give us all things?.

If God spared not His own Son, will He withhold your healing?

If God spared not His own Son, will He withhold the house you want or the car you need?

No. He won't.

He loves you too much to withhold any good thing.

When you realize how much God loves you, you won't have any trouble loving others. You won't have any trouble walking in love, focusing on love, thinking about love, and giving away love. You will increase your capacity for positive emotions that fuel your decisions. You will be in control of your soul.

THE SOUL
{section 1}

[will]

[emotions]

[mind]

I want.

I Want It.
And I Want It Now!

Chapter 9

God does not impose His will on anyone, even though it would be a blessing. It is not His will that anyone perish and go to hell. Yet, He doesn't impose salvation on anyone. In the same way, He won't allow Satan to impose death or cursing on anyone.

The bottom line is that you choose. He has said, "I have set before you life and death, blessing and cursing: therefore choose life" (Deuteronomy 30:19).

That's why soul control is so important. Your choices are determined by how effectively you control the process. And your choices are a result of your mind, will, and emotions all working together.

In the next two chapters, I will focus on your will and how it affects your destiny. Your will is the part of you that says, "I want." And usually, it says, "I want it now!" What you want is reflected by the choices that you make. Everything that has to do with spiritual warfare is over your desires and your wants. The enemy uses unfulfilled desire to generate pressure in your life to get that desire fulfilled. Your success in resisting that pressure is what spiritual warfare is all about.

Everything you would call a temptation, a test, or a trial is the product of unfulfilled desire and the battle about how that desire will be fulfilled.

Think about the battles you've endured in life. If one of them has been financial, then you know the desire to be out of debt, to be free of encumbrances to do what God tells you to do with your money. Your desire for all of this is often unfulfilled because you are still in the process of reaching your goals.

As a result, that longing to be free produces a certain kind of pressure that Satan uses to either cause you to make a wrong decision, or at least a premature decision.

There's pressure in relationships, especially when a relationship doesn't meet your expectations. There are times when we see other people with the kind of marriage we want. We read in the Bible about the kind of marriage we can have, and we become discouraged because all we have at the moment is bickering, pain, and heartache.

Unfulfilled desire. The pressure it generates tempts us to relieve the pressure, but that often causes us to make wrong decisions or premature ones.

In all this, the enemy isn't really tempting you. He's just exerting pressure. As the god of this world, he's manipulating circumstances and people to build more pressure.

The Lord will always attempt to influence you through the real you—your spirit—but He won't impose His will on you.

The choice will always be up to you. Your "will" will always have a choice to make.

TEMPTATIONS, TESTS, AND TRIALS

First Corinthians 10:13 says, "There hath no temptation taken you but such as is common to man: but God is faithful, who will not suffer you to be tempted above that ye are able; but will with the temptation also make a way to escape, that ye may be able to bear it."

The Greek word for *temptation* is rendered in other passages as "tests or trials." *The Amplified Bible* defines it as a "trial regarded as enticing sin." All tests entice you to sin, and the tempter is always Satan.

Nonetheless, many people go through life thinking that they are being tested by God. But James 1:13 says, "Let no man say when he is tempted, I am tempted of God" (NKJV). God tempts no man. He is not the tempter.

God never tests you with sickness, lack of finances, or any other bad situation. Yes, tests come, but not from God.

When they do come, do everything you can to pass them. Just like in school, if you flunk a test, you don't move forward. You don't move up. You stay where you are until you pass the test.

Think of it this way. God knows where you are, so He doesn't need to test you. Testing is merely the enemy's purpose for enticing you to sin.

Remember that temptation and tests come in the form of pressure, which is the result of unfulfilled desire. He's always tempting you to get out of faith. The Bible says that whatever is not of faith is sin, so if Satan can get you out of faith, he can get you into sin. He's always enticing you to say, "It must not be God's will to heal me," or "It must not be God's will to heal everybody," or "God must be using this to test me."

Satan manages to corrupt people's theology by bringing pressure. Because the desire to be healed is so great, many people will do anything to relieve the pressure. They'll even say, "Well, this sickness must be the will of God," and then they'll just accept it as the status quo. It gets the pressure of unfulfilled desire off but it takes them toward death and cursing.

THE COMMON TESTS

First Corinthians 10:13 also says, "No temptation has overtaken you except such as is common to man" (NKJV). We always like to think that no one else has ever experienced what we're going through. We like to think it's the worst thing that's ever happened to anyone.

But the truth is that what you're going through is nothing but what's common to man. The account in Luke chapter 4 of Jesus's temptation in the wilderness shows some of the primary examples of the kinds of tests that come our way—all of which are as common as dirt: "Then Jesus, being filled with the Holy Spirit, returned from the Jordan and was led by the Spirit into the wilderness" (NKJV).

Jesus had to go into the wilderness to pass some tests. That's what the wilderness is all about. It's a place of testing that every Christian passes through. The children of Israel passed through the wilderness just as Jesus did, and the Bible says they are our example.

Though the Israelites' passage through the wilderness represents deliverance from the world's bondage into the freedom of the new birth, the children of Israel didn't get delivered from Egypt right into the Promised Land.

It was a journey.

God had a plan for them—something eye had not seen, ear had not heard, that hadn't entered into the heart of man—just like the one He has for your life.

God had a place for them—a place of victory, contentment, fulfillment, and joy—just like the one He has for you.

But to live out God's plan and get to God's place, they had to pass through the wilderness, and so do you.

Now, from the example of Jesus' time in the wilderness, it doesn't have to be a long time like the children of Israel. Jesus was there 40 days and nights. All the tests the children of Israel failed—that cost them 40 years in the desert and many lives—Jesus passed in 40 days.

How long it takes you to pass the tests is up to you.

We find the first common test in Luke 4:3:

The devil said unto him [Jesus], If thou be the Son of God, command this stone that it be made bread. And Jesus answered him, saying, It is written that man shall not live by bread alone, but by every word of God.

The first common test that we all have to deal with is the demand that your flesh will make on you to be fed—not just food, but whatever it wants. Satan knew Jesus had been fasting for 40 days, and he knew Jesus was hungry. There was unfulfilled pressure on Jesus' body to want food.

Doesn't your body put pressure on you all the time to be fed? Doesn't it want too many sweets and choice foods? Does your body love pecan pie the way mine does? When you slice that pie, heat it up, and put a dollop of whipping cream on top—I can taste it now! That's pressure!

You will never be able to satisfy the unfulfilled desire of your flesh. If you give in a little, it will scream for more. If you give it one piece of pie, it will want two!

If you give it one cigarette, it will want more.

If you give it one drink, it will want more.

If you give it a taste of cocaine, it will want more.

If you give it premarital sex, it will want more.

Your body will always demand something, and then it will want more of it.

You can't live by meeting the demands of your flesh. You have to live by the Word of God.

The second common test that we all have to deal with is our view of and relationship to money and the world. Luke 4 continues Jesus' experience:

The devil, taking him up into an high mountain, shewed unto him all the kingdoms of the world in a moment of time. And the devil said unto him, All this power will I give thee, and the glory of them: for that is delivered unto me; and to whomsoever I will I give it. If thou would therefore wilt worship me, all shall be thine.

And Jesus answered him saying, "Get thee behind me, Satan: for it is written thou shalt worship the Lord thy God, and Him only shall thou serve (verses 5-8).

Satan is the god of this world, and he is always looking for worshippers (2 Corinthians 4:4).

So is God.

God is always looking for people who will worship Him in spirit and in truth, so that He can show Himself strong on their behalf (John 4:24; 2 Chronicles 16:9). He's looking not just for people who will worship Him with their lips, but with their lives. The test of your true worship comes from your commitment to service, such as that described in Luke 16:1-12 in the story of the unjust steward.

God wants faithful stewards, those who truly worship Him.

Faithful stewards use their money to help people get saved. The Bible says that is the least we should do with our money. If you don't tithe and give money to help spread the Gospel, then you've already flunked the money test.

Luke chapter 16 makes it clear that the least we have to be faithful in is seeing our money as a resource to get people saved, and that is basically done by supporting the Gospel.

God goes on to say that if you're faithful in the least, He'll bless you with the true riches. The true riches include the anointing, the power of God, the lofty high calling of God, the peace and joy that's in Him—things money can't buy. True riches will only be yours when you are faithful in the very least which is how you handle your money.

Money (to keep this in proper perspective) is nothing but a medium of exchange that represents the material world. When

Satan talked to Jesus about the world, he could say he was speaking to Him about money as well. When he said to Jesus, "These kingdoms will I give unto you," the kingdoms represented money because the only thing that produces power in the world is wealth. So you can't look at this brand of temptation without thinking money or you will miss the whole point of it.

Satan said to Jesus, "I'll give you authority over all the kingdoms of this earth."

Have you ever heard of a king who was poor?

No, of course not. The king is always the richest man in the kingdom. He controls everything.

Here's how you will encounter this testing every day. The world seems to have so much to offer. It's easy to hoard up a piece of the world for yourself. But God wants us to have a paradigm shift in our thinking and see our worldly resource, money, and natural resource in life as a means of getting the Gospel preached, of getting men and women saved, and the kingdom of God increased.

This is what our view of life should be.

If you had been the rich young ruler in Mark chapter 10, would you have sold everything, given it to the poor, and followed after Jesus? Would you have passed the test?

If the world has a hold on you (if money has a hold on you), you'll be tempted to sin. You'll be tempted not to tithe.

The tithe says this: "Lord, I submit my interests in this material world to You, to my interests in You."

But if you hold back, even just a little, you will find yourself confronted with the pressure not to tithe. You'll be enticed to sin. You'll flunk the money test and not be able to promote the Gospel financially.

The third common test that we all have to deal with is tempting God. Tempting God? Yes, tempting God. It is equally important to obey God and abide by His Word and to do it with the right motive. Luke 4:9-12 illustrates this:

> He [Satan] *brought him* [Jesus] *to Jerusalem, and set him on a pinnacle of the temple, and said unto him, If thou be the Son of God, cast thyself down from hence: For it is written, He shall give his angels charge over thee, to keep thee: And in their hands they shall bear thee up, lest at any time thou dash thy foot against a stone. And Jesus answering said unto him, It is said, Thou shalt not tempt the Lord thy God.*

Tempting the Lord is the same thing as testing the Lord. Testing the Lord is when we do something just to see if it is really going to work. It's when you do what the Word says but not necessarily from the heart. You do it with an attitude that says, "Well, we'll just see if the Word really works in this area."

I've seen people do this with finances. It's as though their attitude is one that is challenging God, daring Him to move. Their reason and motivation is all wrong. They're trying to manipulate God. I've seen people in financial straits go to the extreme. They'll just clean out their bank accounts (their grocery money, mortgage payment, and so on) and give it all to the church saying, "Okay, God. I give it all. You say if I give, it's given unto me. Well, I'm just trusting You."

No, they're not! They're tempting (or testing) God.

People do it with other things besides money. They think if they go to prayer meeting two extra times this week, or spend a longer amount of time in their devotions that maybe God will do something for them.

Those are all good things, and God wants you to be involved in good things, but always for the right reason.

When you tempt God, isn't it a root of unbelief? Isn't it acting out of the frustration of the flesh?

When you're in faith, you give because you *know* God will take care of you, not because you're hoping to bribe Him. When you're in faith, you are confident in what God will do for you. You know you're His child. You know He loves you—and you love Him. You're secure in Him. You understand that anything not of faith is sin.

The first generation of the children of Israel died in the wilderness because of unbelief and because they tempted God.

If you tempt God in the wilderness, you will lose those goals and dreams you're striving for. You have to stay in faith and truly trust God and His plans for you.

All three of these tests, trials, and temptations are experiences you'll face in life. What you do with them makes all the difference. Your will has to be in subjection to your spirit, so that you make the right choices. Your will always wants something, and it will want it now! The pressure on your flesh because of unfulfilled desire may seem unbearable at times—but it really isn't. The greater One lives on the inside of you. Resist the pressure and yield to what your spirit is telling you is right. Don't yield to making the wrong decision or a premature decision. You'll only regret it if you do.

YOU CAN PASS THE TEST!

Remember 1 Corinthians 10:13? We studied the first half; now let's gain understanding concerning the rest of the verse.

God is faithful, who will not suffer you to be tempted above that ye are able.

He will always make a way for you to escape! That's good news! God won't let Satan turn the pressure up to the point you can't bear it anymore. Yes, there will always be people who buckle under the pressure. It's because they did what Galatians 6:9 describes—they got weary and fainted. But they didn't have to. God is saying He will never allow the enemy of your soul to give you more than you can take. You always have the capacity to resist the pressure—and when you resist the pressure, he leaves!

First Corinthians 10:13 gives us this assurance:

But will with the temptation also make a way to escape, that ye may be able to bear it.

Everything you ever have experienced or will experience has a way of escape. God always provides a way of escape from defeat, failure, bankruptcy, death, infirmity, humiliation, reproach— anything and everything.

So what is the way of escape? James 1:2 says, "My brethren, count it all joy when you fall into various trials." No matter whether it's a test or temptation having to do with your body, your money, or a heart issue, you can count it all joy if you know the next verse; "…knowing that the testing of your faith produces patience. But let patience have its perfect work, that you may be perfect and complete, lacking *nothing*" (NKJV, emphasis mine).

Satan's testing is designed to entice you to sin. The testing of your faith is just his ploy to entice you away from what you have decided to believe. But the experience of going through the test works something into your life called patience, and when patience has her perfect work, you come out the other side of the test perfect and entire, wanting nothing (James 1:4). Perfect and entire means whole and complete.

If you go through the tests of life and maintain consistency, you will make it! Consistency means not changing in the face of pressure. The enemy is applying pressure to get you to change, to waver. But you must learn to control your soul and be consistent about it.

Your warfare is to remain steadfast on the Word of God, never reacting and making decisions under pressure, and God will perfect that which concerns you. God will order your steps. God will see to it that you always triumph in Christ.

Supernatural
Pressure Relief

Whether we realize it or not, all too often we do things that increase the pressure on our lives. We inadvertently place ourselves in more pressure than we want. Obviously, we don't really want to do that, and God doesn't want us to either.

God wants to help us relieve the pressure. He wants us to enjoy life—even when we're going through the tests, trials, and temptations. The Bible is full of ways we can relieve the pressure to ease our way through the wilderness and to the end of our faith.

Much of what we have covered thus far in this book is designed to do just that. I want to succinctly look at these basic principles from the perspective of relieving pressure so your will can succeed and have a greater chance of cooperating with your spirit.

THINK THE RIGHT THOUGHTS

Renewing your mind is something we've already talked about in this book. It's the process of adopting the value system of the Bible and standard of behavior that comes from God's Word. And we have seen that spending time renewing your mind with new knowledge isn't complete until your feelings begin to change as well. Feelings are the most powerful motivators of human behavior.

So to truly renew your mind, you not only have to adopt a new standard, you also have to change the way you feel about things.

Feelings. They have everything to do with pressure relief.

How you feel about something or someone either turns up the pressure in your life, or turns it down. If you think about the negative aspects of your test or trial long enough, you will go down the road of, "I don't know if I can stand this anymore." You will dwell on the downside of your circumstances and focus on the negative potential ramifications. What are you doing? Turning up the pressure.

And we all do it.

We tend to think about the worst-case scenario. We prepare for the worst. The enemy isn't the one turning up the pressure. Satan isn't attacking us. We're doing it all by ourselves just by what we're choosing to think about!

Increase the pressure or decrease it—you have the power to control the pressure just by what you think.

Philippians 4:6-8 tells us what to think:

> *Be anxious for nothing: but in everything by prayer and supplication, with thanksgiving, let your requests be made known to God. And the peace of God, which surpasses all understanding, will guard your hearts and minds through Christ Jesus* (NKJV).

The peace passes all understanding because the circumstances that generated the pressure haven't changed. So it passes all understanding that you should obtain peace at all.

Isn't God good? Peace is available to you, instead of pressure, even when everything is falling apart around you.

Verse 8 begins with "finally":

> *Finally, brethren, whatsoever things are true, whatsoever things are honest, whatsoever things are just, whatsoever things are pure, whatsoever things are lovely, whatsoever things are of good report;*

if there be any virtue [and this word means "power"] *and if there be any praise, think on these things.*

In other words, don't waste your time thinking on things that are lies. Don't think on things that are untrue. Don't think about the misrepresentations that have been made about you. Don't think about how you've been treated unfairly. Don't think about the racial difficulties. Don't think about your old lifestyle. Don't think about the sexual options outside of marriage. Don't think about the dishonest, deceptive, deceitful things that have been done or said or that you'd like to do in return to people.

Renew your mind with the Word and think about what is pure, think about what is lovely, think about things in life that bring you joy, things that produce peace in your heart.

Flying helps me to think on those things. Over the years, I have flown thousands of flights, but there are certain flying experiences I've had that when I think about them, they bring an unmatched peace and satisfaction to me. I remember one time when I was in the Air Force flying F101s, I had come off a single ship mission and I was alone. The puffy cumulus clouds were enticing. I spent 15 minutes doing barrel rolls, loops, and Cuban 8's. It was an exhilarating, private experience. It was awesome. When I think back on that, it brings me peace. It brings a place of joy to my heart.

If you want the peace that passes all understanding, get your mind off the stack of bills. Get your mind off the doctor's report. The Bible says to think on things that are of a good report. When you do, it will turn the pressure down, not up.

Speak the Right Words

Another way to relieve the pressure in your life is to speak right words. Words are ideas, concepts, and paradigms of life. They are perceptions of reality. They are seeds sown into the soil of the human heart that have the capacity to change the human experience.

So what are you hearing? And then speaking?

As I have taught in other chapters, words are the way you bring your thoughts captive. More importantly, what I want you to see and understand is how they relieve pressure. Speaking right or wrong words will either decrease the pressure or increase the pressure you will have to contend with on the way to the end of your faith.

Ephesians chapter 6 tells us that the Word in our mouths is the sword of the Spirit. Jesus exercised His sword of the Spirit in the wilderness. Despite how intense the pressure was, He used His words to decrease it.

Another way your words can relieve pressure is by speaking words of praise. Hebrews 13:15 says:

By him therefore let us offer the sacrifice of praise to God continually, that is, the fruit of our lips giving thanks to his name.

If you're in the pressure cooker right now, start praising Him—aloud! Sing, shout, talk, whatever it takes. Give Him thanks. If you will, I guarantee you, as you focus on God and His greatness, your pressure will decrease.

Try speaking edifying words to others—instead of venting. Ephesians 4:29 says we are to be ministers of the grace of God, speaking words that build others up.

Building others up decreases your pressure! Think about it. Think about the last time you and your spouse had an exchange. Was it edifying? Did it minister grace? Did it build your relationship up?

If it was encouraging, then it decreased your pressure.

If it was a heated exchange, then it increased your pressure.

If you couch it in words that edify, if you communicate in a way that builds up and ministers grace, then you decrease your pressure.

The bottom line is this. If you don't communicate well with everyone in your life, it will produce pressure you'll have to bear.

Revelation 12:11 says that we overcome by the blood of the Lamb and the word of our testimony. That means we need to testify about what God has done in our lives. Our testimony, together with the blood of the Lamb, is what makes us overcomers. Being mindful of what God has done in our lives relieves pressure.

That's what David the shepherd boy did. When he faced Goliath (talk about pressure!), he talked about the lion and the bear he had slain. He knew the power of his words. He said to King Saul, "The Lord that delivered me out of the paw of the lion, and out of the paw of the bear, he will deliver me out of the hand of this Philistine" (1 Samuel 17:37). When it came time to put up or shut up, he ran to meet Goliath.

Proverbs 18:21 says there is the power of life and death in the tongue. God has told us to choose life or death, blessing or cursing. The way we choose is to speak.

So speak life. Speak blessing. Speak the Word of God. Speak praise and thanksgiving. Edify. Minister grace to others when you talk. Testify of all the good things God has done for you.

LANGUAGE TO AVOID

Just as you have all the power in the world to speak right words and to speak in right ways, you also have the power to speak wrongly.

For the rest of this chapter, I want to clue you in to some seriously wrong ways you can speak, ways which will surely increase the pressure in your life, produce vain imaginations, and lead to wrong choices.

The apostle Paul says in 1 Corinthians 13:11 that when he was a child, he spoke as a child, and acted as a child. The most significant way a child speaks and acts is that his entire universe is centered around him. He knows nothing else.

So the first wrong way to use your words is to talk about yourself. This is the most common way people generate pressure on themselves without even being aware of it. To talk about yourself from time to time isn't harmful, but if you are the topic of your conversations on an ongoing basis, then it is.

As a rule, when we talk about ourselves, we do it in either one of two veins: we either talk about ourselves in a way that lifts our esteem in the eyes of others, or we talk about ourselves in a way that generates sympathy. Both of these are pressure generators.

Proverbs 27:2 says, "Let another man praise thee, and not thine own mouth; a stranger, and not thine own lips."

The way you get the pressure off of you is to become concerned about someone else.

The second way to speak wrongly is to complain or murmur. That means no whining or griping, either! Don't do it in the little things, and don't do it in the big things. Don't do it in traffic. Don't do it about your husband or your wife. Just don't go there!

Philippians 2:14 says, "Do all things without murmurings or disputings."

First Corinthians 10:10 says, "Neither murmur ye, as some of them also murmured, and were destroyed of the destroyer."

Complaining will turn up the pressure quickly! That's because murmuring, complaining, and griping are rooted in unbelief. They are a quick way to get over into testing God. It's a way that you critically appraise God—and that's dangerous to do.

When you magnify the source of your complaint, you are turning up the pressure—and you're turning up the heat on yourself.

I know it is so tempting to talk about what you're going through and how bad it is. I know that is our tendency as humans. But Jesus set the example for us. In Isaiah 53:7, His behavior was prophesied:

He was oppressed, and he was afflicted, yet he opened not his mouth: he is brought as a lamb to the slaughter, and as a sheep before her shearers is dumb, so he openeth not his mouth.

Jesus went through the greatest test any human could ever go through, and He never griped or complained. He never opened His mouth. Neither you nor I have ever had it as tough as He did, so why do we feel we have to open our mouths? God knows what you are going through, and He's the only one who needs to know.

When things are not going well, that's when you need to turn your attitude around. That's when you need to get on the uphill side. That's when you need to generate a little joy. Resist the desire to mope around and put on your saddest puppy-dog eyes. Don't let people see the darkness trying to engulf you. Don't be manipulative by trying to look like something is wrong so others will ask you if something is wrong.

Using your words in wrong ways only increases the pressure.

Learn to use words the right way to relieve your pressure. Help your will to succeed by making the right choices.

The third way you can use your words wrongly is talebearing—repeating something negative that you have heard. Proverbs 11:13 says "a talebearer reveals secrets, but he who is of a faithful spirit conceals a matter" (NKJV).

When you listen to or spread talebearing, you are being used of Satan to increase pressure in someone else's life. When you say that the Holy Spirit told me to tell you about someone so you could pray, you are being used by the enemy.

The Bible says a man's harvest depends entirely on what he sows. If you sow talebearing which increases negative pressure in people's lives, then that is what you will reap—increased pressure in your life that you will have to bear.

The last use of wrong words I want you to understand is speaking words that create division, contention, and strife. Any words that divide or polarize the body of Christ are wrong uses of words. Romans 16:17 says:

> *Now I beseech you, brethren, mark them which cause divisions and offences contrary to the doctrine which ye have learned; and avoid them. For they that are such serve not our Lord Jesus Christ, but their own belly; and by good words and fair speeches deceive the hearts of the simple.*

People who create strife and division always sound good. They use good words and fair speeches, but when you measure the effect of their words, it does not create harmony or unity. They generate strife and contention that grows like a spiritual cancer. God says to "mark them" and avoid them.

You Can Make It!

God wants you to endure to the end of your faith. He's equipped you with ways to relieve the pressure and win the tests. He's given you ways of escape so you can come out on top. God is for you.

You have a free will. You can choose life and blessing or death and cursing. Apply the principles of this chapter and choose life. You really can make it all the way to the finish line!

Your Supernatural Source of Comfort—The Holy Spirit

God knew we'd need help learning how to get comfortable in times of testing, trials, and temptations. He knew we'd need some supernatural assistance to get above the pressure and to really see our circumstances through God's perspective and through God's eternal love and faithfulness. So He gave us the Holy Spirit, our Comforter whom helps our will succeed beyond what we would be able to endure on our own. John 14:16-18 says:

> *I will pray the Father, and he shall give you another Comforter, that he may abide with you for ever; even the Spirit of truth; whom the world cannot receive, because it seeth him not, neither knoweth him: but ye know him; for he dwelleth with you, and shall be in you. I will not leave you comfortless.*

We have a supernatural force of comfort that unbelievers don't have. We don't have to live tormented and so pressured that we quit before we get the answer, or toss in the towel and say, "I can't handle it anymore."

We have a helper, the Holy Spirit, and we need to understand how to receive from Him.

LISTEN FOR HIM

The Holy Spirit comforts us so we can cooperate with Him and receive the end of our faith. He does this by first bringing us into remembrance of God's Word, either the written Word or something He has spoken to us. John 14:26 says:

The Comforter, which is the Holy Ghost, whom the Father will send in my name, he shall teach you all things, and bring all things to your remembrance, whatsoever I have said unto you.

The Greek word for *remember* used here means "to put in mind." The Holy Spirit will put in your mind words of life that will help you in the test you are in.

But most people are so consumed with the problem at hand, that they miss the promptings of the Holy Spirit. Because they aren't tuning in, they miss what He's saying to them. When the doctor gives them another bad report in the middle of an already serious illness, they don't hear Him saying, "By the stripes of Jesus, I am healed." Every time the doctor explains how bad it is or how bad it's getting, they don't hear the Holy Spirit speaking. They just hear the doctor.

In every situation like this, the Holy Spirit is speaking, trying to redirect your focus to help you stay grounded on the truth, even as you deal with the facts. He's trying to bring God's truth to your remembrance to help relieve the pressure you're feeling, so you can be clear minded enough to make good and sound decisions.

But you have to listen for Him. You have to be tuned in. We have to train ourselves to always be listening for His guidance and comfort.

WALK IN THE FEAR OF THE LORD

Another way the Holy Spirit helps us is to lead in the direction of recognizing how big God really is versus the size of our problem. Acts 9:31 says:

Then had the churches rest throughout all Judea and Galilee and Samaria, and were edified; and walking in the fear of the Lord, and in the comfort of the Holy Ghost, were multiplied.

In this passage, walking in the fear of the Lord and in the comfort of the Holy Spirit go hand in hand. When you are filled with reverential awe of God, of His greatness and goodness, of His mercy that endures forever, it causes a prostration of your heart before Him. And that's what the fear of the Lord really is—and it is extremely comforting. It's comforting to recognize in your heart whom you are serving and that you are a member of His family.

Those moments when the greatness of God overwhelms your senses, it makes your problems come into perspective. Suddenly He becomes much bigger than any problem you face. You become aware not only of His goodness and greatness, but more importantly, you become aware of His desire to display that goodness and greatness in your life.

Moments like this are a realization that you are under His wing, in the shadow of the Almighty. He is your refuge and fortress. It encourages you to cooperate with Him and for problems in your life to begin having solutions.

FORGIVE THE PRESSURE AWAY

The Holy Spirit also brings comfort by leading us to forgive those who have wounded us because forgiveness relieves pressure. Second Corinthians 2:7 says:

So that contrariwise ye ought rather to forgive him, and comfort him, lest perhaps such a one should be swallowed up with overmuch sorrow.

There is comfort in forgiveness. Yes, if you've forgiven someone, it does bring comfort to them, but it also brings comfort to you. Your willingness to forgive brings comfort to you, because as Mark 11:25 says if you're not willing to forgive others, God can't forgive you. So when you extend forgiveness, you enable God to forgive you, and comfort follows forgiveness.

One of the surest ways to increase pressure is to harbor unforgiveness. One of the surest ways to release it and receive comfort is to extend forgiveness.

Philippians 2:1 says there is comfort in love. There is comfort for those who are the object of your love, but also for you. When you make a decision to love someone, comfort comes to bear in your own life.

And here's the bonus to all of this. Deep down, you can't really do any of these things on your own. You can't prophesy, walk in the fear of the Lord, forgive, or love on your own. The Holy Spirit helps you do all of that. But He operates through your expectation, cooperation, and faith.

GIVE IT AWAY

Lastly, as you are filled with comfort, like everything else God fills you with, give it away. Give someone else comfort. Second Corinthians 1:3-5 says, "Blessed be God, even the Father of our Lord Jesus Christ, the Father of mercies, and the God of all comfort; Who comforteth us in all our tribulation."

The power God gives us never flows independently of His purpose. God never empowers you to do your own thing. He empowers you to fulfill His purpose. Giving to others what He has given you is always His purpose.

So if you ever want to retain something, give it away. He doesn't comfort you so you can be a comfortable couch potato. He comforts you so you can comfort others. Verse 4 goes on to say:

We may be able to comfort them which are in any trouble, by the comfort wherewith we ourselves are comforted of God.

God intends for you to have supernatural comfort during your tests and trials so the pressure doesn't get too much for you to bear, so you can make it to the end, perfect and entire, wanting nothing. Therefore, He comforts you in all your tribulation. And then He expects you to comfort others with the comfort you've received.

[will]

[emotions]   # THE BODY   [mind]
{section 2}

Body Language—
What's Yours Saying?

Chapter 12

God created you to be a free moral agent. He gave you the right to make the choices that determine your experience of life, including how you spend eternity. He doesn't violate that freedom, and Satan can't violate that freedom. It's all up to you what you experience in life.

As we have discussed in our teaching on the soul, your choices are a product of the inner action of your mind and emotions. What you think and how you feel produce a decision, an action in the will that falls on either the side of life and blessing or on the side of death and cursing. That's why it's never right to blame others for your failures or shortcomings. Sure you might be married to a real buzzard, or your boss may be the meanest person alive. Your upbringing or socioeconomic status may affect what you can and can't do right now, but everything in the natural realm is subject to spiritual truth if you use your faith to change it. Just because you grew up a certain way or are in a difficult situation right now doesn't mean you or your circumstances have to remain as they are.

Whether you like it or not, you are a product of all the choices you have made, because whoever controls your soul, controls your destiny. So, who's controlling you? You may want to think it's your mother-in-law, but she's not. The truth is there are basically two main possibilities for who might control your soul.

The first possibility for who might control your soul is your spirit which is in contact with God. It is possible for your spirit to control your soul, and if that's the case, God would be able to get His direction and His plan through to you, thereby enabling you to walk down the path of His perfect will for your life.

The second possibility is your body, which is driven by sensory perception of everything external, everything that is in this world. If your soul is controlled by your body, which is controlled by the world, which is controlled by Satan (who is the god of this world)—you're in a heap of trouble.

Because Satan is the god of this world, he has the legal right to manipulate both people and circumstances to make situations seem favorable that really aren't. He has the power to feed you information in order to persuade you to make decisions based on worldly input. In other words, he has the power to deceive you, working through your body.

The essence of this truth is this: God can—with your cooperation—control your soul through your spirit, and Satan can—with your cooperation—control your soul through your body.

WHO'S DOING THE TALKING?

When it comes to God's Word and understanding what it says about how we're to live and behave, it's an open-book test. The answers are written out for us very clearly. We're not to murder, steal, or commit adultery. We're to honor God and our parents. We're to love our wives and honor our husbands. But what are we to do about choosing careers or deciding whether to move to the East Coast or the West Coast? What are we to do about choosing the right school for our children?

That's where we have to learn how to listen to the voice of the Holy Spirit. We have to learn how to discern when it is the Holy Spirit speaking to us and when it's our own bodies. We have to figure out who's doing the talking! Is it God or our bodies?

"You mean our bodies talk?" Yes. We could call it body language—and everyone has it. First Corinthians 15:47 says:

The first man is of the earth, earthy; the second man is the Lord from heaven.

Man was made from the dirt of the earth. In the book of Job, it refers to mankind as clay.

The Amplified Bible version reads this way; "The first man [was] from out of earth, made of dust (earthly-minded); the second Man [is] the Lord from out of heaven."

Mankind is by nature "earthly-minded." Our bodies talk about nothing except earthly things. They always talk about what they want.

Verse 48 goes on to say:

Now those who are made of the dust are like him who was first made of the dust (earthly-minded); and as is [the Man] from heaven, so also [are those] who are of heaven (heavenly-minded).

So our spirit talks to us about heavenly or spiritual things and our body talks to us about earthly things. Our bodies don't have the capacity to talk to us about godly things. When we take the time to think about the wonders of creation, or what eternity has in store for us, or the awesomeness of God, what we think about doesn't come from our bodies. Our bodies don't have the capacity to generate those kinds of thoughts. Our bodies talk about going fishing or playing golf. Our bodies want to watch TV and do those things that please the body—earthly things.

Now, just because your body only talks to you about earthly things doesn't mean those earthly things are wrong. Sure, some might be. They might be destructive or dangerous to your well-being. But things like watching TV or playing golf are obviously not wrong endeavors.

The point is that for you to hear the Holy Spirit concerning God's will for your life and all the decisions you have to make on a daily basis, you have to discern when your body is talking and when your spirit is talking—and then choose which one you're going to follow.

Your spirit will always talk to you about spiritual matters and the greatness of God. It will always lead you in the direction of God's will for your life. There will even be times when your spirit and your body will get into alignment and agree. But in general, your body will never talk to you about God, even though God made your body.

He made your body to work for your good. It's part of His creative purpose. God made your body to recognize hunger, so you wouldn't starve to death. He made you to have a sexual drive for the propagation of the species. There are areas where the spirit and body do agree. God wants you to eat. He wants you to reproduce (only after you're married, of course).

The problems arise in our lives when our spirit and body don't agree, when there's disagreement and confusion about who is saying what.

YOU'RE JUST A BAG OF DIRT!

Knowing your body's language is the key to discerning between which voice is doing the talking. Your body can only talk about earthly matters. It's just a bag of dirt, and that's the only way it can think.

Romans 7:24 records Paul's lament over the negative pull of the body:

O wretched man that I am! Who shall deliver me from the body of this death?

Calling his body a "body of death" has a biological application and a spiritual application.

Spiritual death is separation from God—when your body talks, it never takes you toward God.

Because your body is dead to God, it is doomed to biological death. From the moment you were born, your body began a decline leading to death. Of course, this is a period of growth and development, but the truth remains that the biological clock starts ticking when you enter this world.

God didn't originally create mankind this way. Mankind was intended to live forever in the Garden of Eden. But Adam sinned and blew it. Adam was told to eat of the tree of life, but he didn't. He disobeyed and ate of the wrong tree. So God in His mercy moved Adam and Eve out of the Garden so mankind wouldn't live forever in a sinful state. God got man out of the Garden before he ate of the tree that would have made him live forever in a tainted condition.

So the legacy Adam passed to us all, including the apostle Paul, is a body of death that has no capacity to take us toward God.

When you awoke this morning, your body began talking right away. "Oh, stay in bed. You're tired. You can be a little late to work today."

Your body will never coach you to get to work early or to never miss church or to pray before your feet hit the floor in the morning. Your body will tell you to turn on the morning news and have that cup of java. It will always look out for itself! When you are weighing and measuring out the pros and cons of a situation to make a decision, your body will always put up an argument for the natural side. Romans 7:23 says it clearly:

But I see another law in my members, warring against the law of my mind, and bringing me into captivity to the law of sin which is in [my body].

Not only do you have a body of death, but you also have a body that conforms to a law that will always result in disobedience to God. Your body just doesn't have the capacity to obey God. The law in your body insists you go the opposite way from God. The decisions you let your body talk you into will always take you away from obedience to God.

Are you "body ruled" or "spirit ruled"? Galatians 5:17 says, "For the flesh lusteth against the Spirit, and the Spirit against the flesh: and these are contrary the one to the other: so that ye cannot do the things that ye would."

Then Paul goes into the works of the flesh, which if your body dominates your life, then these kinds of attributes will typify your behavior:

> *But if ye be led of the Spirit, ye are not under the law. Now the works of the flesh are manifest, which are these; adultery, fornication, uncleanness, lasciviousness, idolatry, witchcraft, hatred, variance, emulations, wrath, strife, seditions, heresies, envyings, murders, drunkenness, revellings, and such like: of the which I tell you before, as I have also told you in time past, that they which* do such things *shall not inherit the kingdom of God.*
>
> Galatians 5:18-21

The Greek word for *do* in the phrase *do such things* means "to practice." So if you slip up now and then, that isn't going to keep you out of the kingdom of God. But practicing the works of the flesh will. Practicing the works of the flesh is living body ruled, and if you live long enough that way, at some point, you will choose to reject Jesus.

But in this passage, Paul is talking to Christians, those who are saved and in the Church. He's warning them and us to beware of practicing the works of the flesh, because it leads to not inheriting the benefits of being part of the kingdom of God.

The Amplified Bible translates the works of the flesh as "...immorality, impurity, indecency, idolatry, sorcery, enmity, strife, jealousy, anger (ill temper), selfishness, divisions (dissensions), party spirit (factions, sects with peculiar opinions, heresies), envy, drunkenness, carousing, and the like."

What catches my attention in this translation is "selfishness." Selfishness is definitely a characteristic of body language. Your body will always talk to you about you. It gets up in the morning thinking about you, planning about you, figuring out how to minister to you, calculating what you can do today to bless you. From morning until night, this is what your body is talking about. The body is selfish, so it talks selfishly. It talks primarily about your needs.

When God talks to you, He focuses on the provision He has already made for your needs and your calling to serve others. He's purchased your salvation, healing, deliverance, and provisions. Thus God's focus is spiritual truth, not the temporal truth that is subject to the spiritual truth.

But that's not the body's language.

The body talks to you about need—you need more money, a better husband, a better wife, a better church, a better car, better kids, and on and on it goes. Everything is wrapped up in you when your body is talking. Your body has no capacity to talk about anything else!

YOUR BODY HAS LOTS TO SAY!

Your body's language is comprehensive. It covers a lot of territory. It has many characteristics. It never talks about God. It always talks about you. It never leads you toward God. It leads you toward the works of the flesh. It doesn't have the capacity to obey God, so it will always lead you down a path of disobedience. And it will always rebel against authority. That's what the "strife and seditions" refer to in the works of the flesh.

In America today, we have difficulty with submission to authority. We've raised generations of kids that mock authority. Perhaps we've taken our liberty too much for granted and failed to realize that the liberties we have and the nation we have is due to godly authority. Godly men laid the foundation of our country and established all the privileges and freedoms we enjoy.

Today, not every authority in power is godly, but according to Romans chapter 13, we are still to honor them and to be subject to them as unto God.

Although the Word explains that all authority is ordained of God, that doesn't mean that God put every man or woman in his or her office of authority. What it does mean is that God established authority so there would be order and not anarchy. He established the offices of authority—regardless of who's standing in those offices.

So whether or not you like the current president of the United States, God requires you to submit to that office of authority. Whether or not you like your boss, God requires you to submit to that office of authority over you.

When you relate to an office of authority correctly—by submitting rather than rebelling—God can bless you regardless of the person standing in that office. You can relate properly to that office by praying for the person in it. Pray for your husband. Pray for your boss. Pray for your city council members. Be respectful of authority and God will use it to produce His will in your life.

But know this: your body will never want to submit to authority. That's not its language.

It's always easy to submit to authority when that authority is smart enough to do what you believe is right. But the moment that authority takes a different direction, and in your opinion, they've made a mistake, your body starts talking coup. It says, "You shouldn't be going along with that. You should let them know you disagree. You should voice your concern and your opposition to what's happening here."

When you let your body rule, then strife and division run rampant. Think about it. Let all I've just written sink in. Think about it in terms of church splits. Never in history was there a church split initiated by God. Never.

Yes, churches have purposely planted another church and part of the congregation has filled it. But that's not a split.

A split is the result of strife. Church bodies not wanting to submit create division that leads to the split—bodies who didn't believe God was big enough to correct leadership when it was the right time.

God has called us to unity, and a body-ruled life will never be able to attain to unity. A body-ruled life will always find fault with what authority is telling it to do.

IT JUST KEEPS TALKING!

Remember the *Lays* potato chip slogan, "Betcha can't eat just one." Well, why can't you? Because your body will always want more! Your body always takes you to excess. That's just another characteristic of its language. When it has something it likes, it wants more and more. If something seems good to your body, there's no end to the demands it will make on you for more and more and more. Almost anything can be done to excess, even good things. The only thing you can't do to excess is spend time with God.

When you give into your body's demands for more and more, what eventually happens? It becomes addicted. It forms habits. God made it that way, but He made it for good things.

He wants you to have good habits, but your body will always crave bad ones.

Habits can be anything—from benign things to destructive things.

The body always falls into patterns unless you train it otherwise.

God wants you to understand how your body talks to you. He wants you to understand body language. He wants you to know its characteristics and weaknesses:

- It is earthly minded.
- It is a body of death.
- Its members operate in the law of sin.
- It is always concerned about itself.
- It doesn't take direction from authority very well.
- It always pushes things to the excess, to the extreme.
- It is a habit-forming body of flesh.

If you understand these truths, you are better equipped to be able to discern between the voice of your body speaking and the voice of your spirit (indwelt by the Holy Spirit) speaking to you.

Who's Really in Charge?
The Real You—or Your Body
{Chapter 13}

My Mom always made the best pecan pie I have ever tasted. Consequently, it was one of my greatest weaknesses. When her pecan pie was around, it's all I could do to just eat one piece. I felt like the apostle Paul as I ate one piece after another: "For that which I do I allow not: for what I would, that do I not; but what I hate, that do I... For I know that in me (that is, in my flesh,) dwelleth no good thing: for to will is present with me; but how to perform that which is good I find not" (Romans 7:15, 18).

It sounds like Paul is into tongue twisters here, but I think you get the message. There are things in our lives that we do, and we know they're wrong—like eating a whole pecan pie!—but we do them anyway! Somehow we feel out of control and unable to stop ourselves.

Why is that?

Because we are "body ruled."

The Amplified Bible says it this way: "For I do not understand my own actions [I am baffled, bewildered]. I do not practice or accomplish what I wish, but I do the very thing that I loathe [which my moral instinct condemns]" (verse 15).

It's the human dilemma. Romans chapter 7 describes the body-ruled Christian. Body-ruled Christians care about what they are doing wrong and wish they could do something differ- ent, but they just can't. Of course, for unbelievers—all of which are body ruled because they have no other option—there is no other way. The only source of information they have is in the world in which they live.

But Christians have the Holy Spirit living on the inside of them. When they do wrong, they know it. It's like sandpaper on their insides. They don't want to do wrong. They just feel power-less to change—even though the truth is they do have the power. They just haven't learned how to use it.

So, Who Is Ruling You?

We all have areas of our lives that are body ruled, because none of us will be perfected until we go home to be with the Lord. But our objective is to get those areas back under subjection to our spirits. We want to get progressively better as we mature—which is very possible. God wants us laboring constantly to improve and make our bodies servants to our spirits, instead of vice versa. I want to help you better understand what it means to have areas of your life "body ruled" by giving you some examples.

One of my personal weaknesses (besides my Mama's pecan pie) is losing my temper—especially in traffic. If I'm running late and someone cuts me off—well, let me just say it's not a good scene in my car. Why is it that I have overcome in my life more areas than I can count but this is such a problem for me? It seems to happen over and over again in my life. I know I shouldn't get aggravated. The other guy is probably running later than I am. I know I should speak a blessing over that person who just cut me off, but I don't. I feel bad about it. I wish I didn't do it. After it happens, I always think about how I wish I had his license number so I could track him down and call and apologize for my rude behavior. I tell myself, "I'm not going to do this again!" But then somehow, somewhere, the same guy shows up next week! And I fly off the handle again!

Why is that? I don't want to be this way!

I'm sure you can relate to my feelings. We all have areas like this.

Another example is people overeating. We blame it on our thyroid, our metabolism, or our circumstances. But the bottom line is that if you take in more than you burn up, you gain weight. And it's not just the visibly overweight people who do it.

I've done it. But because I run, it doesn't show up on my body. But eating all of my Mama's pecan pie was definitely overeating. Anytime I've overeaten, I've always felt rotten about it. I knew I shouldn't have done it, and I tell myself I won't do it again, but eventually, I do.

There's no logic behind this kind of behavior. It's completely out-of-control behavior. It's living body ruled!

BODY RULE LEADS TO DEATH

Life doesn't have to be this way. Living out of control, yelling at other drivers, overeating, abusing your wife, screaming at your children, living with addictions—none of these things are okay. If you're making excuses for yourself saying, "I won't do that again," you will—unless you take some active steps to prevent it.

I know I've kept this truth a little light talking about my Mama's pecan pie and all, but the truth is I want you to understand how out of control our bodies are. The fact is if you allow your body to rule in any one area, it will creep into other areas of your life as well. There is no such thing as maintaining the status quo where your body is concerned.

I remember a friend that I went to college with. When we were young, neither of us had much interest in the Lord. We lived our lives for ourselves. We both partied hard. Then, one day, he met a beautiful Christian girl, filled with the Holy Spirit. They fell in love and he decided she was worth changing for. So he quit smoking and drinking and running around. They married and he became a devoted husband.

Well, I didn't have contact with him for about 25 years. Finally, one day when we re-established our friendship, I learned they had divorced. My heart ached because they had been so perfect for each other.

When I asked him how it all transpired, he explained that it started with insignificant things. He remembered how at one point, he felt so much pressure from the office, that he lit a cigarette for the first time in 12 years. Then a day or two later, he had another one. Then a week or so later, he was having two a day. Then, eventually, he was smoking as regularly as he once had.

Because he associated smoking with drinking, it wasn't too long until one afternoon he stopped for a beer on the way home from work. Days later that one beer after work became two. Soon, those two stops became daily stops, and eventually, he was unfaithful to his wife.

The truth this progression reveals is this: if you don't stop your body from controlling you, then it will take you down a slide toward death. In this case, it was the death of a marriage.

According to Galatians 5:21, those that practice the works of the flesh (meaning they let it become a pattern in their lives) won't inherit the kingdom of God. In other words, if they don't correct a body-ruled pattern of behavior, ultimately it will cost them all the benefits being a child of God provides.

So you can't allow your body to rule and control you.

YOU CAN CHANGE! I CAN CHANGE!

The truth is you don't have to be in bondage to your body. There are ways to break your body's rule and control over your life. I've discovered four ways that I believe will help you change.

If you will do them, you will control your body. I know they've helped me change in immense ways.

The first is this: uncontrolled or undesirable behavior is always rooted in a misbelief which has established a vain imagination or stronghold. No, I don't mean unbelief. I mean misbelief. Misbelief is when you believe something that isn't true, whereas unbelief is refusing to believe the Word.

The reason I can say that body-ruled behavior is always rooted in misbelief is because it's the truth of God's Word that sets you free from bondage. God's truth brings liberty to every part of your being.

Now, I believe the Bible. I believed all the verses that directly addressed my temper and even my overeating, but that didn't stop me from doing those things. Believing the Bible didn't change my thinking. Why is that?

Psychologists have a good suggestion that I believe is valid. It's consistent with God's Word. Psychologists make the point that all deliberate behavior is preceded by something called an internal monologue or self-talk. I believe this is valid because as a believer, I know that internal conversation is occurring between my spirit and my body.

Don't think it's so? Then start listening to yourself. Before you engage in wrong behavior, stop for a moment and listen to the self-talk in your head. It will reveal the misbelief that is at the root of your wrong behavior.

An example of this in my life is my temper. The Word says I'm to have a cool spirit. I'm supposed to be easy to be entreated, gentle, and kind. Yet, I find myself aggressive, overbearing, trying to convince someone that I'm right, all the while in my head I'm talking, "I know I shouldn't be doing this! Why am I doing this?"

I remember the first time I stopped to listen to my self-talk during a heated conversation. I remember the guy I was talking to and what we were talking about. But I stopped and listened to what was inside of me. I knew the Bible said that love never fails. Be gentle. Be kind. Give soft answers. I knew all that. But deep down, I realized that I believed that if I could let enough anger show, that if I could intimidate someone just a little, I could get my way quicker! I really believed that because that's what my self-talk was saying. I believed that if I let just enough anger and aggression show, I could avoid a useless conversation. And that was wrong.

So how do you and I correct our misbeliefs?

First, we identify them.

While I was eating the first piece of pecan pie, my self-talk was justifying the second. My spirit said to me, "You'll be sorry!"

But my body said, "It isn't going to hurt. One piece won't matter."

My spirit responded, "You know you'll end up eating the whole stinking thing!"

But my body argued, "You can run an extra 10 miles tomorrow."

My spirit countered, "You know that's just glossing over the problem."

My self-talk of going back and forth about eating a piece of pie demonstrated that my behavior was predicated on the misbelief that it would really be okay.

My pecan pie dialogue is the same trap an alcoholic fights: "One drink isn't going to hurt. I can handle this."

So the next time you're torn between doing what is right and what is wrong, stop and listen. What is your self-talk saying? What you hear is a clue to identifying your misbelief and an indicator of where in the Word of God you need to go deeper and grow more mature.

Why did I keep getting mad at the other guy on the freeway? Because I believed he deserved it. That was my misbelief. The truth that set me free—I'm controlling my soul now!—was that God says vengeance is mine. Judgment is His. It wasn't my job to punish unruly drivers!

Listen to your self-talk. Identify the misbelief, and then deal with the vain imagination or stronghold it has propagated by applying the principles of soul control we have taught you thus far.

BE THE BOSS

The second way I believe you can change is to show your body who is the boss. You do that by practicing something called "discipline." First Corinthians 9:25-27 says:

> *And every man that striveth for the mastery is temperate in all things. Now they do it to obtain a corruptible crown; but we an incorruptible. I therefore so run, not as uncertainly; so fight I, not as one that beateth the air: But I keep under my body, and bring it into subjection: lest that by any means, when I have preached to others, I myself should be a castaway.*

The Greek root word for *temperate* means "self-control." So the Lord is saying in these verses that if you're going to succeed in what He's called you to do and in what He's called you to be, you'll have to be self-controlled in every area of your life.

You simply can't turn a deaf ear or a blind eye to your weaknesses, whether it's overeating or losing your cool. I realize there may be a lot of things in your life that need correcting or adjusting, but God doesn't expect you to fix them all overnight. He does, however, expect you to correct what He brings to your attention. You know what He has highlighted in your life to work on, so just deal with that. When you overcome, He'll show you something else. Step by step, you'll get to where you need to be.

That's how you grow in God and eliminate the body control that takes you away from God. You have to see that your body is not the real you. A lot of people never make that distinction. They look in the mirror and think what they're seeing is real, but it's not. It's just a bag of dirt! Remember? God made you from the dust of the earth. You wouldn't want a "dirt bag" controlling your destiny, would you? Of course not.

The real you is a spirit. That's who we want controlling our lives.

First Corinthians 9:27 says, "I keep under my body, and bring it into subjection." Subjection to what? to whom? You bring it into subjection to your spirit, the real you.

In *The Amplified Bible*, verse 27 says, "But like a boxer, I buffet my body." That means you handle it roughly, discipline it by hardships, and subdue it. That means you are to be the boss!

That's how people were at the turn of the 20th century. Obesity wasn't a problem because people walked everywhere they went. Their bodies got handled roughly because there weren't the conveniences and technology we have today that allow for alternatives. They got plenty of exercise. My dad walked between five and seven miles to school. My mom walked three miles to the grocery store.

Today in America, everyone shuns discomfort like it was a plague. But Paul is saying in 1 Corinthians, you can't do that. You have to treat it roughly. You have to buffet your body. You have to train it like a boxer does for a big fight. He gets his body in shape. He doesn't step into the ring and knock out his opponent having never trained.

Like a boxer, you have to subject your body to hardship to get it into submission. It has to be trained to be in submission to your spirit.

Paul's analogy to a fighter is a critical spiritual truth. Everyone—including you—will some day have to be in the ring fighting a major battle. It's just a fact of life, whether it's physical, financial, or relational, there will be lots of battles along life's journey.

The good news is that if you live your life according to the Word of God, you can win at every one of those battles. If you buffet your body so you aren't body ruled, you will have the stamina spiritually to stand in that day.

Deny your body what it wants, just to keep you in charge. Make it suffer. Fast different kinds of foods or activities from time to time to keep it in subjection. Say "no" to yourself. It reduces self-interest and amplifies the will of God in your life. It amplifies your ability to hear what God wants. That's the true definition of Christian suffering—making your body know who is boss!

TALK TO IT—STRONGLY!

The third way you can control your body is to talk to it and tell it what to do. James 3:2 says, "For in many things we offend all. If any man offend not in word, the same is a perfect man, and able also to bridle the whole body."

How do you offend not in word? You only say what God says about you, about others, or about your circumstances. Verses 3-5 go on to say:

Behold, we put bits in the horses' mouths, that they may obey us; and we turn about their whole body. Behold also the ships, which though they be so great, and are driven of fierce winds, yet are they turned about with a very small helm, whithersoever the governor listeth. Even so the tongue is a little member, and boasteth great things.

You have the ability to bridle your body if you talk to it. So speak to your body. You tell it what to do. Put words of faith in your mouth and speak life.

I've learned to talk to my body when I'm running. Through that, I'm controlling my body. I tell it, "You're not going to get tired. You think you're going to quit? You got another three miles to go!"

What do you need to be saying to your body? Get bold! Tell your body what it's "going to do" and tell it what it's "not going to do." Tell it, "You are not going to eat any more of this food. You are not going to stay in bed. You are going to pull yourself out of bed, put on your shorts, and go running. You are not going to watch TV right now. You are not going to sit there like a couch potato. You will get into the Word of God. You will put on a CD. You will worship."

Does any of that sound like something you should start saying?

Talk to your body and tell it to line up with the will and Word of God. If you will, you can turn your body as a bit in a horses' mouth turns his whole body. You can live ruled by your spirit and not your body.

Take control of your body. Identify the culprit of misbelief. Discipline your body and say, "No" to it. Talk to your body. Let the Lord tell you what it is He wants you to do with your body and your life.

Remember Joshua 1:8 says, "This book of the law shall not depart out of thy mouth." Keep the Word of God coming out of your mouth. Talk to your body for your behavior will always follow your mouth and your mind.

Also, remember the law of the mind says if you renew your mind to the Word of God, you will be transformed. It is a miraculous transformation to walk out the perfect will of God. This is how you present your body as a living sacrifice. This is how you get your body under control.

[emotions]

[will]

[mind]

THE SPIRIT
{section 3}

Finally!
The Real You

{Chapter 14}

Renewing your mind, intensifying godly emotions, remaining consistent under pressure, disciplining your body— all these things are steps toward controlling your soul. But there's one final part of you to understand before you can fully grasp what soul control is all about.

Your spirit.

Have you ever been faced with a decision and said, "I just wish I knew if this was God" or "I wish the Lord would come in a burning bush and tell me the right thing to do"? You want to do the right thing, but you can't seem to figure out what God is telling you to do.

That's why it is so important to understand what your spirit's role in controlling your soul is. When you understand your spirit— the real you—you can let God be fully in control of your soul.

I want to show you how you can better understand which voice is God's voice, which direction He is leading, and how your spirit plays a role in your daily decision making.

WHAT DOES GOD WANT FROM ME?

You've probably noticed that the Word describes the general will of God for all believers of all ages. It shows each of us how to live, but it doesn't go into specifics for our individual lives. It doesn't tell you where to live, who to marry, or what vocation to pursue. How do you find that out?

In these specific matters, the Holy Spirit provides direction to you through your spirit.

I know that, you may be thinking, *but how do I know which direction comes from Him and which comes from my own flesh?*

Hebrews 4:12 provides us with this key:

For the word of God is quick, and powerful, and sharper than any two-edged sword, piercing even to the dividing asunder of soul and spirit, and of the joints and marrow, and is a discerner of the thoughts and intents of the heart.

The word *soul* here refers to the soul without spiritual input. You could also call this the leading of the flesh because that's the only other source that will provide direction if your spirit isn't engaged in the process. We're being told that the way to discern between what is you (your flesh) and something that is really from God (through your spirit) is the Word of God.

So the Word of God doesn't provide specific direction for your life, but it gives you guidance on determining specific direction?

Yes! Although it may initially seem contradictory, these things are different. The word that the Holy Spirit speaks to you is from the Greek word *rhema*, which is often translated as "word" in the Greek New Testament. But Hebrews 4:12 uses a different form; "word of God" can actually be translated to "logos." Essentially, this scripture is saying the written Word of God will always show you what is a *rhema* word from the Holy Spirit. The written Word and the principles in the written Word will always make a clear distinction between what is spoken to you by the Holy Spirit and what is spoken to you by your flesh.

This process of dividing between the soul and the spirit isn't an easy thing to do. The writer of Hebrews likens it to dividing between bone and marrow. If you know anything about biology, there really is no dividing line. Inside of a bone, the hardness of the bone gradually decreases. It gets softer and softer and softer until it's marrow in the center. There really isn't any clear division. And he's saying that sometimes dividing between the leading of the Holy Spirit and fleshly desire is that difficult.

There's only one way you can do it. If you truly want to be led by the Spirit, it is a necessity to read and study the Word. You can't pray enough, you can't confess enough Word, you can't go to enough church services. You need to learn the Word so the Holy Spirit can bring it to your remembrance in order to guide you down the right path for your life.

That is one of the Spirit's jobs—to bring to your remembrance Scriptures that will divide between soul and spirit. When that happens, the written Word acts as a two-edged sword that will divide clearly between flesh and spirit.

I'll give you an example. You might say to me, "I have a job offer in Seattle. How do I know if I should move there? I love the geography there, the climate, the hunting, and the fishing. I've even got friends and relatives there. It seems like God's telling me to move there."

Sounds pretty good, doesn't it? Certainly, there's nothing in the Word that counters moving to Seattle. You say, "I feel good on the inside about moving to Seattle, so it must be God."

Wrong!

Yes, it could be. But the only way you'll know is for the written Word to make the division between the soul and the spirit. As you pray about this opportunity, the Holy Spirit might bring Hebrews 10:25 to your remembrance which talks about "not forsaking the assembling of ourselves together." He might empha-size to you through your spirit the word *forsake*. As you meditate on that, you may begin to sense that the Holy Spirit is telling you to not forsake the assembling of yourself with the current church body you are in for being with friends and family in another city. You aren't to forsake it for a better climate, hunting, and fishing. Maybe you aren't to forsake it for a better job opportunity.

Yes, you might have an *itch* to move to Seattle. But the Spirit has brought a Scripture to your spirit that your mind has latched onto and the understanding of it has come.

Though Seattle looks great, sounds great, and feels great, that urge in your heart to stay connected with your current church is the Spirit directing you down the right path. Moving to Seattle wouldn't be God's will for you. If you choose it, you'd be making a wrong decision.

What if you're trying to decide whom to marry?

There is no chapter and verse in the Bible giving you the name of the person you're to marry, so you have to get that from the Holy Spirit, right?

Let's say you're a young handsome fellow at church one Sunday morning and this gorgeous gal comes into the service. Immediately you say, "That's my wife! I know it's God's will."

You make an effort to spend time with her and find out that the two of you agree on what's important in life. You like the same food, hobbies, etc. It seems like the right thing to get married. But how do you determine if the Holy Spirit is leading you to marry or if your flesh is pushing you that way?

The Word tells us many things that should provide an answer. First of all, the Word says not to be unequally yoked together with unbelievers (2 Corinthians 6:14). When you are initially considering someone as a marriage partner, that question needs to be answered first. Is he or she a believer? You'd never imagine how many times people have found "the perfect man for me" or "the perfect woman for me," but that person doesn't even know God. Both of you need to be a Christian.

But you can't stop there. Being unequally yoked doesn't simply refer to somebody being born again. It also refers to yoking yourself to someone who has the same understanding of the Word that you do. If you believe that God is a good God who heals, prospers, sets free, and delivers, and you marry someone who believes the opposite ("Well, you know, you don't know when God's going to hammer you. He may just make you sick every now and then to teach you a lesson"), you're going to have problems. The Bible says that two can't walk together except they be agreed (Amos 3:3). The most basic agreement of all has to be regarding the Word of God.

If all the natural things show that you should marry so-and-so, check the Word. It will divide your soul and spirit, and provide you with principles that will show you the direction you should take.

IN RING NUMBER 1: SPIRIT VS. FLESH

Day in and day out, a lot of people let their flesh direct their lives, until they realize what they are doing and repent. After repenting, they don't necessarily change anything to be better led of the Spirit. Or they forget about the Spirit until they come to a crisis situation, and then they want to hear what He has to say.

So the question truly becomes, how determined are you to walk in the Spirit? Because if you're not determined to walk in the Spirit, you will wind up in the flesh by default. Romans 8:13 shows the result of that; "For if ye live after the flesh, ye shall die." That's about as final a conclusion as you can have. You will die spiritually, physically, and biologically if you live by the flesh.

Living by the flesh is habitually doing those things listed in Galatians 5:19-21:

Now the works of the flesh are manifest, which are these; adul-tery, fornication, uncleanness, lasciviousness, idolatry, witchcraft, hatred, variance, emulations, wrath, strife, seditions, heresies, envyings, murders, drunkenness, revellings, and such like: of the which I tell you before, as I have also told you in time past, that they which do such things shall not inherit the kingdom of God (KJV).

"But, Mac, I thought salvation was based on grace, not works. These verses make it sound like a works program."

I went over this principle in chapter 12, but I think it would be good to revisit this important Bible truth. The key to understanding this text is the Greek word for "do" which is *prasso*, and it means "to practice, especially repeatedly, or habitually."

We all get in the flesh sometimes and make mistakes, and an occasional sin won't keep you out of the kingdom of God or from obtaining its benefits. This portion of scripture is referring to the person who habitually practices the works of the flesh; it is their lifestyle, not an occasional misstep.

As I said before, the key is being deliberate to walk in the Spirit, so you don't default to living in the flesh. The result of living after the flesh is death. Simply put, your flesh will take you down the road to destruction.

It wouldn't happen all at once (you wouldn't drop dead the moment you step into the flesh), because death is always a process. Death seldom occurs in one fell swoop. As long as you walk after the flesh, your life in this natural arena will be a downhill slide of cursing and death.

God tells us to mortify the deeds of the body and we shall live. For as many as are led by the Spirit, they are the sons of God (Romans 8:13-14).

It's not enough to be born again. To maintain your status as a believer, you have to live your life being led by the Spirit. Romans 8:17 goes on to say, "...if children, then heirs; heirs of God, and joint heirs with Christ."

Being led by the Spirit is something that should occupy your consciousness every day. It has to be a part of you at all times. When we come across decisions each day, we should ask ourselves, *What is my soul saying and what is my spirit saying?* You should always live tuned in, listening, and running every decision by the voice of your spirit, which is being led by the Holy Spirit.

GET RID OF THE ROADBLOCKS

As you begin living your life led by the Spirit, it's important for you to be aware of various obstacles to hearing the voice of your spirit. They are hindrances you will have to learn to overcome if you're to be successful at making decisions for life and blessing—and they are all things you know.

Obstacle #1: Pressure

As you've already learned, pressure is one of the ways the enemy tries to influence you. He's the god of this world so he has the legal right to manipulate circumstances and unwitting people to generate pressure in your life. You've also learned that you should never make a decision with the primary goal of relieving pressure, because that decision will usually be one for death and cursing.

Oftentimes, when the financial pressure is on, people will file for bankruptcy or borrow money to relieve the pressure. In certain circumstances, bankruptcy or borrowing money may be the right thing to do to get out of an impossible place, but most of the time, it's not the answer. God has a better way of solving your financial difficulties.

Most marriages that end in divorce do so because divorce was the result of relieving the pressure of a failing relationship. Again, there are times where divorce is allowable, and it is certainly not the unpardonable sin many in the body of Christ make it out to be. But most of the time, divorce is man's alternative to doing the right thing, which is aligning your behavior with scriptural truths regarding marriage.

Whatever kind of pressure is coming against you, with God's help, you can overcome it. You don't have to yield to the enemy's temptation to relieve it. Make the determination to be led by the Spirit rather than being led by pressure.

Obstacle #2: Fear

God says in His Word that He's not given us a spirit of fear, but of power, love, and a sound mind (2 Timothy 1:7). Yet, fear is a real factor in the lives of many people. Ultimately, prolonged fear will produce one of two things: panic or paralysis. The enemy wants you to become paralyzed with fear, anxiety, or worry. He wants you to panic and run.

For that reason, do not make decisions when fear is present in your life. If you make a decision out of fear, it will be a decision that will lead you toward death and cursing every time. It will always be the wrong decision. First overcome the fear; once it's gone, then make your decision.

Fear can wear many masks. One common display of fear is worry. If you tend to be a worrier, then focus on trusting God and eliminating the worrying and fretting, because it will skew your decision making.

Obstacle #3: Anything that robs you of your peace

Yes, you have to overcome fear and pressure. But really, you have to overcome *anything* that robs you of your peace. If the Lord says to be led of the Spirit and follow after peace (Colossians 3:15, AMP), then anything that robs you of your peace is going to throw you off track. It's something you have to overcome.

Anything that keeps you upset will keep you from being led by the Spirit. Don't make decisions when you are upset.

Being upset, angry, frustrated, or in a hurry are all "peace thieves." If your desire is to be led by the Spirit, you must overcome them.

Obstacle #4: Tendency to rebel against authority

Another tendency that our flesh must overcome is its proclivity to rebel against authority. I mentioned this in a previous chapter, but it is important to remember because much of the leading of the Spirit concerning corporate matters will come through channels of authority. All of us will have multiple experiences in our lives when we will not agree with the decisions made by authority figures. You may think they're making a horrible mistake. It may be inconvenient for you. You may want to go the other way. But here is a truth that we cannot ignore. God, very often, leads us through the authority of leadership in our lives. And whoever you're submitted to is your authority.

Everyone has someone in authority over them. Children have their parents. Adults have employees. Families have pastors. And when I say submission, I'm not talking about blind obedience to someone. No, submission to authority is a heart issue. It's an attitude that says, "I understand that where there is more than one person, God uses established orders of authority to bring direction in corporate matters. Therefore, I will esteem and respect whatever source of authority is in my life. I will not do this solely because the man or woman in that office is worthy of my esteem or respect, but because that is God's order and leading in my life in the way of His will."

If you will esteem the positions and offices above you and if you will pray for those in authority, you can expect the leading of the Lord to come through them where they have power over your destiny.

Think about it. If you have an unbelieving boss, yet you honor him and do your job to the best of your ability, he will be inclined to give you a promotion or a raise when the opportunity arises. That's God directing your life through authority.

That's God blessing your obedience to His Word and overcoming your tendency to rebel against authority.

That's you being led by the Spirit.

Obstacle #5: Selfishness

Watchman Nee ([1903-1972], a native of China who was born again in 1920 at the age of 17 and became a prolific minister of the Gospel and writer) once wrote that our spirit is God conscious, our body is world conscious, and our soul is self-conscious. How true. Without the influence of the spirit, your soul will be self-conscious. You will always be concerned about you, your agenda, and what is best for you. You won't be concerned about the welfare of others as much as you are concerned about your own—all of which is a sure sign that your flesh is leading your life.

As I talked about earlier, God wants you to live your life directed outward, toward the concerns of others. He wants you giving to others, thinking of others, looking out for others. He wants you to be a vessel used to benefit other people. He wants you to do whatever you can in order for people to come to know Him and to experience His fullness.

To do that, you'll have to overcome selfishness. You can't be led by the Spirit and be selfish at the same time. The two don't go together.

Obstacle #6: Impatience

Impatience is another obstacle we must learn to overcome if we are ever going to be led by the Spirit. Impatience is that tendency we have to jump in and do something ourselves when we don't think God is responding quick enough. If you are one of those people who has a tendency to not be able to wait, then you will have to work on this one especially hard.

Brother Kenneth Hagin ([1917-2003] founder of Kenneth Hagin Ministries and Rhema Bible Training Center, Tulsa, OK) made it a practice to allow himself at least two hours before a service to just sit and wait on the Lord. He didn't pray. He simply waited.

God wants us to talk less and wait more. We need to learn to let the Lord have His timing about some things. When we see something we want, we have a tendency to want to make it happen. We feel like we can't live without it—whether it's a godly thing or something else.

But if we'll learn to wait on the Lord, if we'll give Him an opportunity to redirect, to correct, to instruct, to strengthen, and refresh, we'll walk in the Spirit and get all the right things in the perfect time. If we don't give Him these opportunities, it's highly unlikely we will consistently be led of the Spirit.

If you'll overcome these six obstacles, you can move closer than ever before to living your life led and directed by the Holy Spirit. However, nothing is gained without a price being paid; everything in life that is worth having costs something. And the more precious something is, the more it costs.

Your flesh will have to pay a big price in order for you to be led by the Spirit. But what you have to look forward to is worth the price: contentment, satisfaction, peace, being perfect and entire wanting nothing.

The Foundational Key
to a Spirit-Controlled Life

Identifying what is your spirit and what is your flesh is the first step to living a Spirit-controlled life. Unfortunately, that's not all there is to it. There have been times in my life (and I'm sure in yours as well) when I knew the will of God, yet I still yielded to my flesh.

Perhaps the anger level rises to a high point in a confrontation with another person. I know I'm to be calm, and respond with a gentle answer. I know what the Word says about loving and preferring your brother. But sometimes I let my flesh have its way and I respond in an ungodly manner.

All of us have these types of examples where we know the will of God, but find ourselves responding to the flesh instead of the spirit.

I asked the Lord if there was something that would help us gain more control over our lives and ultimately be Spirit-led Christians. Maybe there was a key that would help us follow the Spirit's voice and step away from our flesh.

The Lord opened my understanding to this with a general statement. "How can you be led of the Spirit if you don't even know the general direction the Spirit's going to lead you?"

So the next step to being Spirit-controlled is to have a correct paradigm (or perception) of life, one that matches the direction the Holy Spirit will always take. In other words, there is a particular understanding of life that will orient you in the right direction, the direction of the Spirit.

Jesus talks about this proper orientation in Mark 4:26-29:

And he said, So is the kingdom of God, as if a man should cast seed into the ground; and should sleep, and rise night and day, and the seed should spring and grow up, he knoweth not how. For the earth bringeth forth fruit of herself; first the blade, then the ear, after that the full corn in the ear. But when the fruit is brought forth, immediately he putteth in the sickle, because the harvest is come.

The kingdom of God operates on this life principle: the principle of sowing and reaping. The seed of something is planted, it grows up, and harvest follows.

In verse 13, Jesus said, "Know you not this parable? How then will you know all parables?" If you don't understand the principle of sowing and reaping, you're not going to get anywhere. It is key to experiencing the harvest that God wants to bring into your life.

If you're going to be led of the Spirit, you're going to be led on the basis of what it means to be a sower and a reaper in the kingdom of God.

UNEARTHING TRUTHS ABOUT SOWING AND REAPING

Before we can fully grasp what this perception of life should be for us, we need to understand what seed is and what soil is. Jesus answered these questions in verses 14 and 15 when He explained the parable to His disciples. The seed is the Word of God. The soil represents the human heart.

Many people assume seed is money, but that's a wrong perception. You can't sow a dollar bill in somebody's heart. Seed is not things either; you can't sow a car into somebody's heart. (I'm not suggesting we don't give people material things. Giving in that fashion can be a wonderful demonstration of God's love.) A seed reproduces after its own kind. Material things are not seed. Money is not seed. Spiritual seed is the Word of God that is sown into the soil of the human heart.

In reality, spiritual seed can be considered any kind of idea, philosophy of life, or concept. Weed seeds (thorns) are ideas or concepts not based on the Word of God. Good seeds are those ideas about life that originate from the Bible; an example would be the idea that God heals His children. Weed seeds come from the mind of man; an example would be the ideas from the famous book *Winning Through Intimidation*. If either of these ideas take root inside someone's heart, a harvest will come, based off that idea.

Galatians 6:7 shows us why these things are important to understand:

> *Be not deceived; God is not mocked: for whatsoever a man soweth, that shall he also reap.*

I like what the Phillips translation says; "A man's harvest in life depends entirely on what he sows."

We must have this paradigm of life to position ourselves to be controlled by the Spirit.

How does sowing and reaping translate into our daily living? Ideas (seeds) are going to be sown into your heart by other people. You can't sow into your own heart; somebody else does the sowing. You can water (cultivate) the ideas you receive, but you can't sow them. Godly ideas will come to you through reading the Bible, hearing the Word being preached, or sometimes through a conversation with someone else.

You can water these seeds by continuing to hear the right ideas and by keeping the garden of your heart free from weeds (worldly ideas that will choke out godly fruit). As you tend the soil of your heart, eventually your heart will produce fruit from that seed. You'll see healing in your life, because the Word was sown in your heart. You'll see financial increase, peace, joy, love, a harvest of godly characteristics.

Seed has been planted in your heart, you've cultivated it, and a harvest of godly things has manifest. This is the starting point to understanding sowing and reaping. But Galatians chapter 6 said that your harvest in life depends entirely on what you sow—and you haven't sown anything yet!

So what do we need to do to be a sower?

Take the harvest in your life and plant it into somebody else's life.

God wants us to bear fruit in our lives so someone else can partake of the harvest. When joy, peace, or financial increase come, these things are for somebody else. God's purpose for our lives includes serving other people so someone else can partake of your fruit.

This is why the Bible says that our lives are written epistles (2 Corinthians 3:2-3). When the Word of God begins producing change in your life and you get around somebody that needs peace, they notice you have it and they need it. When you get around someone that has no joy and you're bubbling over a little bit, it almost bugs them. But they're drawn to it.

People say, "Wait a minute. The Word has brought this increase to me. I can't hold on to it?" No, God says that you'll get your harvest somewhere else. You have to be willing to give the harvest the Word has produced in your life.

In return, God will use other people to bring your harvest to you. No, He won't drop a bag of money on your head out of heaven. He'll use people to bless you. If you've been faithful to let people partake of your fruit of peace and joy, there's going to be a day when you need to be encouraged and God will make sure people are lined up to encourage you.

If you are only interested in hearing enough Word so you can get healed or have a little extra money in your pocket, your fruit is going to die on the tree. Fruit is never intended to sustain the life of the tree that produced it. (An apple tree doesn't live off its own apples.) By definition, it is for someone else to partake of.

We're written epistles of the goodness of God when the godly fruit our lives produce are available for others to enjoy. The peace, love, joy, patience, gentleness, the harvest of fruit that comes after you cultivate the seed of God's Word in your heart—all of this fruit is for others.

Let your joy affect somebody else. Let your peace encourage another person. They'll be partaking of your fruit.

And guess what? There's seed in that fruit. Every time people partake of fruit in your life, you're sowing spiritual seed into their hearts.

Now you've become a sower of the Word of God. You are set up to receive a harvest.

EXPANDING YOUR FIELDS OF HARVEST

Most of the time the body of Christ has heard about sowing and reaping only as it relates to money, but I'd like to clarify that understanding. The Bible only uses the terms sowing or reaping as it relates to money when money is being used to spread the Word of God. (Remember the Word is the seed, not money.)

For instance, look again at Galatians 6:7:

Be not deceived; God is not mocked: for whatsoever a man soweth, that shall he also reap.

Verse 6 establishes the context for this verse; "Let him that is taught in the word communicate unto [that means to give or financially support] him that teacheth in all good things." Verse 7 specifically is used within the context of money and money being used in this particular way.

It costs money to get the Word preached, whether we're talking about nowadays, two hundred years ago, or back when Paul wrote Galatians. It could be providing a preacher with food to eat and clothes to wear or buying air time for a television program or supporting missionaries on the mission field or sponsoring outreaches that minister the Word; whatever it is, it takes money to spread the Gospel. That's why Paul encouraged the Galatians (and us today) to financially support the person who is teaching you in good things.

Who is that person? Who should be teaching you all good things? The local church. Our supply of finances helps our church accomplish the assignments God has given to it for the purpose of reaching the community, city, and nation. That's where God wants your resource principally used.

However many lives you've touched with the Word of God, the truth of God, and with God ideas, is going to determine how many fields God can bring your harvest from.

You may think, "That's not fair because the preachers have an advantage, especially those who are on TV. Look at the millions of people they are reaching with the Word." Don't get too carried away on that train of thought. Many passages in the Bible make it clear that you are entitled to the same reward as the one that preaches. Your financial support makes it possible for preachers to do what they do; you are entitled to the same harvest that they receive from spreading the Word to their congregation and audience(s).

As you are faithful to use your life's resource, both money and time, to support the preaching of the Gospel, you have a share in every life that particular ministry touches. That includes local outreaches, missionaries overseas, television ministry—everything that ministry supports.

A farmer can't harvest a field that he hasn't sown. He harvests where he has sown. The same is true for you. The size of your harvest depends on how many fields you've sown in. As you sow money into the church and keep the Gospel going forth, you are planting seed and preparing fields for you to harvest.

You can also be a sower of the Word simply by speaking, preaching, or sharing the Word with other people. If somebody is sick and the Holy Spirit gives you an opportunity, go up to him/her and say, "I have good news for you. My hands have healing in them; I'd like to pray for you." As you share the Word, you're sowing seed into that person's life.

All of these ideas can be classified as a number of different things: service to others, servanthood, preferring your brother, loving each other, giving. The principle remains the same—live life turned outward, not inward.

God says His kingdom works entirely on this principle.

The meeting of human need is the highest call any of us have. The highest way to meet human need is by presenting them with the Word. The Lord uses physical blessing, such as sending blankets to children in India, as a reward or bait to open them to God's Word. Jesus fed the 4,000 because they had been with Him for three days and they were hungry. And so He blessed them. God is a rewarder.

God will also use blessing in order to draw people. For instance, healing is a dinner bell. Every time Jesus healed someone, the multitudes went nuts. The principle thing He's interested in doing is positioning people to receive the life of God into their own lives.

Our life is a resource to meet human need, and human need will not get met except by the Word of God.

God is going to lead you in ways that will enable you to become a sower, a person that affects other people with the Word of God in a life-changing way. You can measure every leading you get by that truth. If you don't have this paradigm, you will never be consistently controlled by the Spirit in what you do.

Our call is to use our life the best we can to see to it that as many other people as possible hear the Word of God. Purpose to be a sower, a giver, a server. When you do that—sow the Word of God into multiple lives—you're entitled to a great harvest.

Never Look Back

We've established the general direction that the Spirit leads. The next question we can ask is this. Is there a general direction where the Spirit will *not* lead you?

Philippians 3:13-14 tells us the answer:

Brethren, I count not myself to have apprehended: but this one thing I do, forgetting those things which are behind, and reaching forth unto those things which are before, I press toward the mark for the prize of the high calling of God in Christ Jesus.

The Spirit's leading is always forward, never backward.

That last phrase—"I press toward the mark for the prize of the high calling of God in Christ Jesus"—is the summary of the Christian endeavor. It sums up what we are supposed to do in this life. We are supposed to be "pressers." We all have marks we are to press toward. We all have a high calling, a grand plan God intends for us to fulfill. And there is a prize when you get there.

Most people never internalize this. They look at their lives in light of past experience. They feel average in the masses and don't expect to experience anything grand.

God has said that He has things in store for each one of us that "eye hath not seen, nor ear heard, neither have entered into the heart of man" (1 Corinthians 2:9). For those willing to go for it, a life you've never known or dreamed is possible in God.

But in order to obtain this kind of life, you have to press. The word *press* means "to make maximum continuous effort." The life that is possible in God is not going to come to you while you float around on a little faith cloud, quitting your job, and "living by faith." No, it's a press.

We can't make that kind of press toward our high calling because very often it's so lofty and beyond our imagination, we don't know what to do today to get there. That's why Paul says that he is pressing toward the *mark*. Marks are intermediate goals and objectives that we can press toward. Some marks are general in nature and apply to all of us; these are found in the Bible (the mark of serving others, walking in love, being gentle, etc.). We can press toward these things and they will take us in the direction of the high call He has for our lives.

But then there are specific marks for each of our lives.

Most of the time these marks are witty ideas or inventions, things that God shows you that you are supposed to do in your life. These individual marks also take you to your high calling.

This act of pressing forward in the Spirit is predicated on something Paul emphasizes in the previous verse. Before you can reach forth into what lies before, you have to do what verse thirteen talks about—forget that which is past.

Without realizing it, many people allow their past experience to strongly influence their present decision-making process. Paul says you cannot do that.

Yes, you can learn from your past mistakes. The word *forget* doesn't refer to Holy Spirit amnesia. It simply means to put out of mind. (The clear implication of that definition is that you are the one who controls what you think.)

The leading of the Spirit will never be to ponder or reflect on the past. It will always orient you forward.

Learn some lessons. Make some corrections. But don't dwell on the past. Unhook your mind from the past, so you can progress in the Lord.

The Lord brought to my mind three categories of things that we need to forget about our past. It helps us be a little more specific in dealing with our thought lives and the things we are to put out of mind.

FORGET ABOUT SIN

The first thing that you need to forget about is your sin. This includes all types of sin. God doesn't grade sin as bad, worse, or worst of all. He doesn't distinguish between a white lie and robbing a bank, as we tend to do. It's all disobedience to Him, and disobedience breaks your fellowship with God.

What should you do when you sin? If you're born again, the good news is that you are not subject to, a slave to, or bound by sin. That doesn't mean you'll never make a mistake. We live in an unregenerate body of flesh. We will until the Lord returns and we receive glorified bodies. Unfortunately, until we get out of this place, we'll make wrong choices (hopefully on an ever-decreasing basis).

You can come closer and closer to the example of Jesus, but you're going to need to do what the Bible calls *repent* when you do sin and disobey God. As 1 John 1:9 says, you confess your sin, and turn away from it. That is true repentance. (The grace of God is not an excuse for sin; after you've confessed your sin, you need to make a decision to not do it again.)

Once forgiveness has been appropriated, there's something else yet to be done. Look at Isaiah 43:25, "I even I am he that blotteth out thy transgressions." God blots out our sin. He forgives and forgets—that means removes it completely. This is the blessing that we live under in the New Testament.

Forgiveness always involves forgetting. If God hadn't forgotten, He wouldn't have forgiven. That's a connection we see throughout the Word. So when we appropriate forgiveness by confession of sin, the next step is to forget it.

There's nothing that'll close the door more quickly on the plan of God being realized in your life than a sense of unworthiness or guilt. Guilt can be better defined as sin consciousness. When you dwell (sometimes subconsciously) on your sins, the result is all too often a pervading sense of unworthiness. This keeps many people from receiving the blessing of God; they don't feel worthy to appropriate the anointing in their lives. They feel incapable to do the will of God.

All of us have a call on our lives—a divine plan that requires the anointing of God to fulfill it. If you remain mindful of your past sins, you'll be held back from reaching forth into what lies ahead of you. You won't have faith to appropriate the anointing and step out in the plan of God.

If you've got a particular challenge or an area of your life where you keep missing it, that doesn't disqualify you any more than a single miss if the repentance is genuine. The important thing isn't how many times you go to God and repent. The important thing is that you keep doing it until you get it behind you.

God says He will perfect that which concerns you (Psalm 138:8); He is doing His will and good pleasure in your life. The only thing that will keep Him from doing that is if you don't let go of your sins. If you keep being mindful of it, He won't be able to help you shed it.

Forget your past sins. Allow God to perfect that which concerns you.

FORGET YOUR FAILURES

The second thing you need to forget is your past failures. Failure is similar to sin, but it isn't the same thing. Some failure is caused by sin. Much failure is caused because we didn't listen to God or use wisdom and we did something we shouldn't have done and experienced failure.

Hebrews 10:32 is the one place we are told to think back on our past. "Call to remembrance [that means to put in mind] the former days, in which, after you were illuminated, you endured a great fight of affliction." Remember the times you won. You didn't give up, you saw it through, you passed the test, you didn't quit, you endured and came out on top. Remember these times so you can give God glory for what He's done.

Verse 35 tells us the reason it is important to remember our victories. "Cast not away therefore your confidence, which hath great recompence of reward." Very simply, you should think back on your victories, but forget your defeats. Forget your failures.

Everybody makes mistakes. But what you have to get solid in your heart is that God doesn't make failures. You are a winner.

The only way you will experience failure as a lifestyle is if you begin seeing yourself that way.

Thinking about past failures is very dangerous, yet people often tend to do it. The enemy of your soul wants to remind you of when you've failed to try and slow your momentum in going where God wants you to go. But when you are mindful of failures, it produces a negative expectation for what your future holds.

Ultimately, the enemy wants you to dwell on your mistakes, reinforce the disappointments in your life by repetition, and frustrate your expectancy to receive from God, so instead of expecting good things, you begin to expect the worst. Repeated disappointment produces negative expectation, which robs your faith of an element that is needed to bring the promise of God into your life.

This is why you cannot think about past failure.

Remove from your mind any vision or image of failure and defeat. You cannot look at it. You cannot think about it. Remember the times you've won, the times you've come out on top. Dwelling on your victories instead of defeats will increase your positive expectation for the future; this is a must for you to reach forth into the plan of God.

FORGET THE SIN AND FAILURES OF OTHERS

The third category of past experience is possibly the most significant of all. You need to forget the sin and failure of others. It'll hold you back just as surely as remembering your own failure and sin. Mark 11:24 says:

Therefore I say unto you what things so ever you desire, when you pray believe that you receive them and you shall have them.

Hallelujah, glory to God! That's good news, isn't it? Well, we can't stop reading quite yet. Verse 25 begins with "and." Jesus wasn't finished with His thought.

And when you stand praying forgive, for if you have ought against any, that your father also which is in heaven may forgive you your trespasses. But if you do not forgive neither will your father which is in heaven forgive your trespasses.

The truth is, if you have a problem with somebody, God cannot forgive you.

What does it mean for God not to forgive you of your sin? If God doesn't forgive you, the wages of sin is death. As I mentioned earlier, death is a slow slide. It may start with a little emotional death, sickness in the body, financial trouble. It's a slide that touches every area of your life. The only thing that stops that slide for us is God's forgiveness made available through the shed blood of Jesus.

I believe this is a principle problem for many people who have given up in life, claiming that faith isn't working for them. They see death touching various parts of their lives even though they've confessed their sins before God. They don't realize that unforgiveness is holding them back from receiving God's forgiveness for their sins. That's why death is touching their lives. God can't forgive them until they forgive those around them.

Remember forgiving means forgetting. You can't have one without the other. All too often, I've heard people (especially spouses) say, "I forgive you," but they can then provide a litany of things that the other person has done wrong for the past 20 years.

They've forgiven the person, but haven't forgotten beans!

When we refuse to forgive other people, do you know what we're doing? We're essentially saying that the blood of Jesus is sufficient for God to forgive them, but we don't have to. God won't allow you to reject the power of Jesus' blood to cover somebody else's sin and then try to appropriate it for yourself.

This concept literally extends to what you're thinking about other people. If you like to go over other's failures in your mind (somehow it makes you feel like you're a little better than you might otherwise be), you are playing with spiritual fire. You will get burned.

God uses people to bring things to pass in our lives. He extends ministry to you through people. When you hold somebody else's sin or failure in your mind, you relate to them totally different. You hold over them the failures of their flesh instead of seeing them through the precious blood of Jesus. As a result, you limit your ability to receive God's blessing through that person. You've cut off one of the avenues of ministry God can use in your life.

Even more significantly for you, you make it impossible for God to forgive you and you'll personally begin to experience an ever-increasing touch of death in your life.

The Spirit's leading will always be forward, never backward. Make sure you are orienting yourself in that direction as well.

Forget your sins.

Forget your failures.

Forget everyone else's sins and failures.

And celebrate your victories. Remember the times you conquered. Keep these channels clear so you can hear and receive from the Spirit of God.

Follow the Fire

{Chapter 17}

You've been gifted with unique abilities and talents. God gave them to you so you can fulfill His plan for your life.

We've found out the general direction that plan will take you. You'll serve others; you'll bring the message of God's kingdom further in this world; you'll be pressing forward, not backward.

But how do you find out the specifics of God's plan for you?

More specifically, how does God provide leadership for you so you can experience His highest and best?

This question can be answered by looking at Jesus' ministry. John the Baptist revealed two principle thrusts of Jesus' earthly ministry; the first was in John 1:29 when John saw Jesus walking to him and said, "Behold, the Lamb of God, slain for the sin of the world."

Jesus came, first of all, to deal with the sin problem.

John announced the second prong of Jesus' ministry in Matthew 3:11:

> I indeed baptize you with water unto repentance: but he that cometh after me is mightier than I, whose shoes I am not worthy to bear: he shall baptize you with the Holy Ghost, and with fire.

According to Hebrews 13:8, Jesus is the same yesterday, today, and forever. That means He is still baptizing in the Holy Ghost.

He is ready and willing to baptize anyone who will believe and receive. You're included in that *anyone*!

You receive the baptism of the Holy Spirit just like you do the cleansing of sin. Jesus is your Savior. By faith, you believe and therefore you receive. The same is true with the Holy Spirit. You believe, and then receive. I'll talk more about this in the next chapter.

But Jesus doesn't stop there. He also baptizes with fire. When you receive the Holy Spirit, you also receive the fire of God.

Obviously, this doesn't refer to a literal fire burning. Throughout the New Testament, the fire of God is best defined as fervency or zeal. Zeal can be defined as vehement desire (see 2 Corinthians 7:11).

So when we talk about fire, we're essentially talking about desire. The things that you most strongly desire are the things you burn about. Those are the things you can fan the flames of, what you can become intensely fervent about. These desires indicate the specific direction of God for your life. It shows you where He wants you to go.

The fire of God that burns within isn't casual desire; it's vehement, fervent desire.

Desire is your fire.

You can't follow the leading of the Spirit without following the fire. What did the children of Israel do in the darkness of their wilderness journey? They followed the fire. Where did the fire take them? To their land of promise, a land that flowed with milk and honey.

You have a land of promise waiting for you—a place filled with amazing things that eye hasn't seen and ear hasn't heard (1 Corinthians 2:9). Every believer has a land of promise to walk in, a life available to them now.

True, you'll need to fight some giants and scale some walled cities, just as the Israelites did. But God says He has given you the land. You simply need to obediently follow Him.

In the same way that the children of Israel followed the fire to get there, we're going to have to learn to follow the fire or be led of the Spirit in our daily lives.

Often, you'll hear people teach on the fire of God, and say, "You have to get on fire!" But I think that's an unhealthy perception; the Word makes it clear that Jesus has already lit a fire in our hearts. Fire is already burning within you.

One of the problems we often have is that we'll see people we admire who are on fire or passionate about a particular thing, and we'll try to be on fire about the exact same thing.

For example, our evangelism pastor has a passion for seeing souls come into the kingdom. I don't know anybody who burns more than he does in this area. If you're around him a little bit, you will want to burn like he does.

But if you don't have the same call, you won't burn like he does.

God has put a fire in you that you are to follow. You're not to burn like somebody else burns. Everybody's burning for something different. You need to learn to fan the flames of your own fire and then follow that fire.

This is the way the Spirit leads—through the fire that He's put in your heart.

PRAY OUT HIS PLAN

The first place that we have to be led of the Spirit is in our prayer lives. Before you can walk out the plan of God, you have to pray out the plan.

Prayer is fundamental to your experience of God. Being led of the Spirit every day begins by being led of the Spirit in how to pray and what to pray for. James 5:16 says:

The effectual fervent prayer of a righteous man [or woman] *availeth much.*

(Don't let the word *righteous* throw you off. We don't need to be perfect in order to pray. We simply need to remember that we've been made the righteousness of God in Christ Jesus. When we do miss it, we confess our sin and are cleansed.)

We do need to recognize the prerequisite James mentions that is needed for effective prayer. It's fervency. Your prayer will not be effective if it isn't fervent. That means you need to pray about the things that you have strong desire within you to pray about.

I used to watch my wife as she prayed at the altar, crying and weeping. Since I know how God moves in her, I'd say, "Well, I want to do this too." I'd go up, get down beside her, and do my best to squeeze out a tear or two. It didn't work. Most of the time, it just made me wonder what was wrong with me.

One day I realized that I can be as effective in prayer as Lynne (or anybody else for that matter) if I follow my heart and pray from the strength of the fire that burns within me. There are things I can get fired up about. This is where my prayer needs to go.

Don't get me wrong, there are always things you need to pray about that you don't have a fervent desire to pray for. I'm talking about two different things: obeying the Word and being led of the Spirit. There's a whole range of things we need to be obedient to pray for including our families, those in authority, and the government. These are not items up for debate; the Bible tells us we should incorporate these things into our prayer lives on a regular basis. You need to obey what the Lord directs you to do.

But occasionally when you are praying through these things, you'll pray for something and sense a little flame there—perhaps a desire to pray a little bit longer for that person or circumstance. I encourage you to stay and pray there because there's a thrust of the Spirit in that area. That's what needs prayer at that moment.

All of us have things we always have a desire to pray about because it represents the direction the Spirit of God is taking our lives. My wife, Lynne, always has a fire to pray about certain things, including Israel and the nations. You don't have to jump-start her in these areas.

What I have a strong desire to pray for is different from what Lynne prays for, and it's different from what you desire to pray for.

Sometimes God may urge you to pray in a particular direction that you may not normally have a burning desire to pray about. That's okay; it could be an assignment specific to that day. God will provide a special urgency to pray for it. (That does mean you may try to pray about it the next day, but limited spiritual energy will be there, since it was specific to the moment you had that particular burden of prayer. Don't try to work up something that isn't there.)

I will warn you, you might come across someone who will try to create a guilt trap for you. "If you're not praying for this, you're missing God." "If you don't show up every morning at this time or that time, you're not that spiritual." They want you to be as excited about their fire as they are, but they don't realize that you have your own particular fire that you burn with and are called to pray about.

If you can't do what you do (including your prayers) out of your heart, you will be ineffectual. Let the fire that burns within guide your prayer life.

TRUSTING YOUR DESIRES

The fire inside you isn't meant only to guide your prayer life; it's also how the Lord directs your day-to-day steps. The challenge in being led by the Spirit is learning to trust the desires that are resident in your heart. Most people have a hard time trusting their hearts because they know how often they've had wrong desires. We've all had wrong desires because we live in a body of flesh.

Satan knows the way the Lord has structured things to work. He knows God is generating fire within you in particular areas that gives direction and provides momentum for your life. Satan isn't going to sit still and let that happen. He's going to labor to generate wrong desire through your flesh and through the world. The result is you'll have some decisions to make. Is the desire I'm feeling coming from my flesh or is this something that the Spirit is using to direct my life? Folks often know they've had wrong desires and have missed it multiple times in certain areas. As a result, they don't have confidence to follow their hearts when godly desires are truly leading them in a particular direction.

You have to get to a place where you trust the desires that are within your heart. Even more so, you have to come to a place where you trust that God is big enough to give you the right desires and help correct the wrong desires.

We won't always be able to intellectually figure out whether a desire is right or not. We tend to look at a desire and say, "That couldn't possibly be God." I know of several examples in my own life where that kind of view was proved very wrong.

Back in the 1970s before we started this church, Lynne said to me on several occasions, "I wish you desired the things of God as much as you desire to fly." When she'd say that, it would hit me like "Uh, I do too." We both knew ministry was in our future, but she made a valid observation. The strongest desire in me at that point was flying; it made me feel like it was wrong.

But as years passed, I realized that desire wasn't wrong. Where I was at that point in my life, I was being equipped for my future ministry.

I used to be frustrated because I didn't go to Bible college or seminary; I didn't feel like I was really qualified or equipped for ministry. But the Spirit clearly showed me that the time I spent in the military, aviation, and in business was my time of equipping. That didn't fit the natural idea of ministry preparation, but that's how God wanted to equip me.

I have seen it to prove true. My desire to fly was a good thing, even though it naturally seemed wrong. Flying (and all the opportunities that came out of my flying) prepared me for my ministry.

Ask yourself this question, "What do I truly want to do with my life?"

When you are yielded to God and desiring to do His will, your answer to that question is probably exactly where God is leading you.

Time and again, I see people laboring in a vocational arena that they don't really care for. Perhaps they earned a degree in that field because the economy suggested it would be profitable. Perhaps their interests went in different directions later in their lives. Ultimately, they are at a job that their hearts aren't behind. Sooner or later, they'll need to recognize they will succeed most in life only when they live out the true desires of their hearts.

I've also seen people who try to be extremely spiritual about this. They feel the only thing they should truly desire is to read the Bible for two hours each night, pray for three hours every morning, and only talk using the words *thee* and *thou*.

The truth is God fills our hearts with a lot of different desires. I love to be outside in the woods. I used to get condemned about that until I realized that is a place where God refreshes me and ministers to me. God placed that desire there because He made me and knows what I need. Psalm 37:4 says:

Delight thyself also in the Lord; and he shall give thee the desires of thine heart.

An initial reading of this verse is encouraging. Not only does God give us desires, He also fulfills them.

But there's a deeper level at which you can read this verse. It actually shows you how God leads in your life.

Psalm 37:23 says something similar:

The steps of a good man are ordered by the Lord, and he delighteth in his way.

If you delight in the Lord, He gives you the desires of your heart.

If you delight in His way, then He orders your steps.

These two ideas are synonymous. As you delight yourself in the Lord, He gives you your heart's desires and He orders your steps. He brings direction to your life.

In other words, the way God orders your steps is by giving you certain desires. He puts that fire in you. And He expects you to follow that fire.

AND FIRST PLACE GOES TO...

The Lord's direction in these verses is conditional. You have to delight yourself in the Lord. If you don't delight yourself in the Lord, you don't qualify for this direction.

So how do we *delight* ourselves in the Lord? What does that mean?

Delight means to take pleasure in or find your joy in. In a basic sense, it means God needs to be number one.

For a believer, that shouldn't be too hard. If you've realized the depth of God's love for you and the things that God has made available to you and me, it's not hard to put Him as number one.

What else does *delight* mean? Look at Psalm 1:1-2:

Blessed is the man that walketh not in the counsel of the ungodly, nor standeth in the way of sinners, nor sitteth in the seat of the scornful. But his delight is in the law of the Lord; and in his law doth he meditate day and night.

The person who delights in the law of the Lord is the person who meditates on it day and night. "Day and night" is an idiom that means this is your paradigm of life. It refers to the way you think. You think about life the way God says it is in His Word.

The word *meditate* means to "mentally image." That means if you wake up in the morning with a tickle in your throat, instead of imagining yourself sick, you imagine yourself the way God sees you—healed and whole!

When you delight in something, you think about it. Your thought life goes in that direction on a regular basis.

Do you remember when we talked about how the soul operates? I said that desire is created by the interaction of what you think with what you feel. What you think and what you feel mix together to generate desire. Desire is the basis of all consistent decision making.

God gives you desire when you meditate (mentally image). When you meditate day and night (it becomes a matter of life for you), God will bring you the desires of your heart because you're delighting in Him.

I love the way the Word fits so perfectly together.

When we talk about delight, we're talking about priority. We're talking about keeping God at the top of your list, thinking in line with His Word. As you let that be your paradigm of life, God will give you the right desires.

WHEN IN DOUBT, SURRENDER YOUR HEART

What about the desires in your heart that you're still not sure are right?

Be willing to put it on the altar and say, "God, if this isn't You, please change it."

God is in the business of changing wrong desires.

There came a day when I had to do that with my desire for flying. I had to say, "Lord, I realize that my desire to fly may be out of whack with what my strongest desire should be. I'm putting it on the altar; I'm giving it to You. I need You to change it if it's not right."

The desire for flying didn't leave. But over the next weeks, I noticed a change. Flying came beneath the things of God. That hadn't happened before. Flying was (and is) still a part of who I am, but the desire for the things of God stood above my desire for flying.

This step of surrender can be tough. I didn't want to lay down that desire. I was afraid the desire to fly was wrong, and God would take it away. Ultimately, I didn't want to give it up.

A lot of times, we don't surrender our desires because we think we know what we want. But the best thing you can do for yourself is truly open your heart up and surrender those desires.

"God, I want your desire more than anything else. If what I'm feeling right now isn't right, I want You to change it. I'm open to it being changed. I'm not going to try to perpetuate it. Lord, if this is not right, please change my heart."

If God doesn't change anything, keep on doing what you were doing. You're on the right track. You've just given Him permission to change it if it is wrong, which is exactly what He will do once you open yourself up to it.

LET THE LORD BUILD YOUR HOUSE

What happens after you delight yourself in the Lord? Psalm 37:4 continues, "He shall give thee the desires of thine heart."

He doesn't tell us to go out and make our desires happen. He says He'll give it to you. Too many people identify where they should be going by virtue of the fire that burns within them, and then they go out and make that desire happen. They cut God out of the picture by writing the ending to their story, instead of letting God prepare the path.

Psalm 127:1 says, "Except the Lord build the house, they labor in vain that build it." Those who labor in vain will get something built. You can build a life without the Lord, but you'll be building in vain.

The word *vain* means "empty." How many times have I watched men scramble up the corporate ladder, make a lot of money, but in the process they lose their families? They lose personal integrity and character. They lose a number of good things because they've merely served their own purposes trying to fulfill their own desires.

Labor without God is labor done in vain.

So what do you do once you know where God is directing your life? What's the difference between laboring with the Lord at your side and laboring in vain?

The Lord spoke to my heart and said, "The key is whether or not you're taking the care of it." If you've taken the care of it, you're not trusting Him to build it. You've taken the responsibility of making it happen on your own.

I have seen myself fighting this battle in a variety of ways throughout my life. I remember when our church built the beautiful building we're in now. It was several years in the making, and I had to fight not to carry the care of it.

"Where can I get some more money to pay for the building? Let's figure this out." That's me laboring, taking a care for it.

If I really believe that God's going to do it, I'm going to be cool. I'm going to be rested. I'm not going to be uptight, filled with cares. God wants us to rest in Him, knowing that He will take care of us.

That doesn't mean there's nothing left for you to do at this point. But you don't do more than God has opened the doors for you to do.

The Bible says that God will open doors that no man can shut (Revelation 3:8). If a door isn't opening, then move on. God orders your steps (Psalm 37:23). Just take the next step He shows you. When you come to a closed door and you don't know the next step to take, be patient. God's timetable is always better than ours.

Now if you're taking a care for what happens and you come to a closed door, you'll most likely try to kick it down or figure out a way around it. But the Bible says that when patience has her perfect work, we'll be perfect and entire wanting nothing. When you come to a closed door, wait for the Lord to show you what the next step should be. He'll either direct you somewhere else or open the door.

Like I said, His timetable is better than yours.

Simply put, do your best to live life on the basis of the written Word and follow your heart. Trust God that He will do one of two things. He'll either change wrong desires that have pulled you off track or He'll fulfill the desires that are resident inside of you.

When this is your view of life, you can live life without taking a care.

Commit thy way unto the Lord; trust also in him; and he shall bring it to pass … Rest in the Lord, and wait patiently for him: fret not thyself because of him who prospereth in his way, because of the man who bringeth wicked devices to pass.

Psalm 37:5, 7

Commit your way to God; follow the fire inside. Trust in the Lord, and don't fret. As you do this, what will He bring to pass? The desires of your heart.

Truly, this is what makes life worth living.

Be Filled
With the Spirit

{Chapter 18}

How can you consistently make godly decisions each and every day?

You do it by being filled with the Spirit.

When you are filled with the Spirit, you know the will of God, even in your daily decisions.

Elizabeth, Mary's cousin, was filled with the Holy Spirit when Mary came to visit her.

> *And it came to pass, that, when Elisabeth heard the salutation of Mary, the babe leaped in her womb; and Elisabeth was filled with the Holy Ghost: And she spake...*
>
> Luke 1:41-42

And she spake.

When you're filled with the Spirit, you will speak. When you're filled with the Spirit, revelation of the will of God is there. It may be for you personally or for you to speak to someone else. In verses 42-45, Elizabeth greeted Mary, not out of her own understanding, but out of the revelation the Spirit had given her.

> *And she spake out with a loud voice, and said, Blessed art thou among women, and blessed is the fruit of thy womb. And whence is this to me, that the mother of my Lord should come to me? ... Blessed is she that believed: for there shall be a performance of those things which were told her from the Lord* (verses 42, 43, 45).

Naturally, Elizabeth could not have known these things. She was filled with the Spirit, speaking under His influence. Revelation came, and there was a performance of those things that she spoke.

As Elizabeth pointed out when she said, "Blessed is she that believed," it starts by believing. You must believe that you're filled with the Spirit, that you are speaking by the Spirit, and that the things which are spoken will come to pass. Faith is the undergirding element for everything we do in our walk with God.

When you are filled with His Spirit, you are not only filled with knowledge of His will, a revelation of His will, but you are also filled with the ability to do His will. Speak those things you know in faith, trusting God that He will bring them to pass.

This is the progression we see throughout the Word of God.

THE INITIAL INFILLING

Acts 2:4 records the first time believers were filled with the Holy Spirit:

> *And they were all filled with the Holy Ghost, and began to speak with other tongues, as the Spirit gave them utterance.*

The disciples were speaking. Only this time, they weren't speaking with their understanding; they were speaking in tongues. They had been baptized in the Holy Spirit.

A few of you reading this might get a little concerned at the mention of tongues. You're not sure what to think about this baptism in the Holy Spirit. Just relax and hear what I have to say; I once had questions similar to those you may have.

The baptism of the Holy Spirit is an experience subsequent to the new birth. Don't let any religious teaching tell you that this passed away with the early Church or that you receive all the

Holy Spirit you're going to get when you're born again. Neither of those views is scripturally accurate.

As I mentioned earlier, Jesus is the one who baptizes with the Holy Spirit and with fire (Matthew 3:11). And the Bible says He is the same yesterday, today, and forever (Hebrews 13:8). If He baptized in the Holy Ghost yesterday, He is doing it today, and will be doing it tomorrow. The baptism of the Spirit didn't stop with the New Testament Church.

We also see a number of stories in the book of Acts that show you can receive the Holy Ghost after you have believed. Phillip the evangelist in Acts chapter 8 led a revival in Samaria. Many people were saved, and when the apostles in Jerusalem heard about it, they sent Peter and John down there to lay hands on them to receive the Holy Spirit.

In Acts chapter 19, we see Paul finding some disciples in the upper coasts of Ephesus. He said to them, "Have you received the Holy Ghost since you believed?" They hadn't. He laid hands on them, and they were baptized in the Holy Spirit and spoke in other tongues.

You cannot be filled with the Spirit unless you've first been baptized in the Spirit; it is the initial infilling. Once you've been baptized, you can be continually filled with His Spirit, filled with His revelation, anointing, ability, and purpose.

The Evidence of His Infilling

The Bible says that faith has to have corresponding action. James 2:17 says, "So also faith, if it does not have works (deeds and actions of obedience to back it up), by itself is destitute of power (inoperative, dead)" (AMP).

Tongues, the evidence of the baptism in the Spirit, is your step of faith. Many people ask for the Holy Spirit and wait for the

Lord to attack their vocal cords and make them spout out this beautiful prayer language. No, we ask for the Holy Spirit to fill us, and then trust His Word as we make an utterance in a language we don't understand. Romans 8:26 says:

...for we know not what we should pray for as we ought: but the Spirit itself maketh intercession for us with groanings which cannot be uttered.

Paul is talking about groanings or utterances that cannot be intelligibly articulated—something not in English.

Of course, if you're like I was, you're saying to yourself, "Have you lost your mind?"

No, I haven't. This is the Word of God.

I remember when this guy prayed for me to receive the Holy Spirit. He said, "Now say something. But don't make it in English."

"Hmmm. What do you want me to say?"

"Just make an utterance that's not in English."

So I held up my hands, feeling very dumb, and said, "Uhhh—"

He said, "Come on, put a little more effort into it than that. Articulate a little bit."

"But not in English?"

"No," he replied.

I went, "Uhhh, duh duh duh..."

When you're at this point, your mind is going bonkers. Aren't you glad God doesn't fit within the confines of your mind? If He did, then He wouldn't be God! A lot of people get stuck thinking about how stupid they sound when they utter words other than the English language. But God really does work in this way, as much as our minds may think otherwise.

Tongues is literally defined as the language of men and of angels (1 Corinthians 13:1). It is not something fruitful to your understanding. Sometimes tongues will be another language spoken somewhere on earth. That's the way it was with Peter and the apostles when they came out of the upper room. They were speaking in tongues that were foreign languages; other people understood what the apostles were saying. To those people, it was a sign and a wonder that they heard their own languages. As a result, they accepted Jesus.

Other times, tongues is not an earthly language. You might be speaking an angelic language. Paul also writes in 1 Corinthians 14:2 that when we pray in tongues we're praying mysteries unto God. That's why you have to get your mind off what you sound like, and trust that the Holy Spirit will shape what you say into a meaningful prayer language. A good way to do this is to worship the Lord. Focus your mind on the Lord and say, "Okay, I'm going to worship you." And make a sound. Eventually you'll realize that the sound you're making does have some rhythm and articulation. It does sound like it could be a language.

Praying in tongues is an act of faith.

First Corinthians 14:4 says, "He that speaketh in an unknown tongue edifieth himself." When you pray in tongues, you'll get fired up. You'll be encouraged in the Holy Spirit. That encouragement inside your heart confirms you are following God.

When I began to speak in tongues, it took me a day or so before I realized that I had a flow of language coming from me. The Holy Spirit was praying something through me. Once you realize that in your own life, you'll be encouraged that you are doing the right thing.

If you haven't yet been baptized in the Holy Spirit, I encourage you to believe for it today. Do what works best for you—lock the door to your prayer closet and let the Lord have His way with you. Ask your spouse or a close friend to pray with you. Contact our ministry using the information in the back of this book; we have material we can send you and people who can explain it to you. Whatever you do, believe that the Lord will do what He says—that He will give you the Holy Spirit. Put corresponding action to your faith by making an utterance. Get your mind off what you sound like and begin worshipping the Lord.

You may wonder why I'm emphasizing the baptism of the Holy Spirit so much. The reason is, you can't be filled on a continuous basis, able to make godly decisions each and every day, until you've had the initial experience of being baptized in the Holy Spirit.

I believe that ignorance of this truth is one of the greatest ways the enemy has stolen from the body of Christ. If he can keep a Christian from getting filled with the Spirit, he has cut off that person from their main source of power—the indwelling of the Holy Spirit. And honestly, without the Holy Spirit, that person really won't have a much different experience of life than somebody that's an unbeliever.

BE BEING FILLED

Remember what happened to Elizabeth when she was filled with the Spirit? She spoke a revelation of the will of God. What happened in Acts chapter 2 after the disciples were filled with the Spirit and spoke with tongues?

Peter stood up with the eleven, lifted up his voice, and he began to speak (Acts 2:14). He gave the first Holy Spirit filled sermon! Verse 40 shows us the results of that ministry.

With many other words did he testify and exhort, saying, Save yourselves from this untoward generation. Then they that gladly received his word were baptized: and the same day there were added unto them about three thousand souls.

Do you see the principle? You get filled, revelation comes, the will of God is done. Being filled with the Spirit is the first step toward having the will of God known in your life so the will of God can be done in your life. We see this same principle in Ephesians 5:17-18, "Wherefore be ye not unwise, but understanding what the will of the Lord is. And be not drunk with wine, wherein is excess; but be filled with the Spirit."

Understanding the will of the Lord is connected to being filled with the Spirit.

This word *be* is actually the present continuous sense. The phrase "be filled" is more accurately rendered as "be being filled." It's an ongoing, moment-by-moment thing.

The dilemma that most Christians wrestle with on a daily basis is what God wants them to do in life. They think, *Where is God leading me? Am I supposed to take this job? Am I supposed to spend time on this project?*

As we saw earlier, when you're filled with the Spirit, you're filled with an understanding of the will of the Lord.

But I already am filled with the Spirit and I still don't know His will, you may be thinking.

The first thing you'll want to do is believe that you know the will of God. Secondly, know what it means to stay continually filled with the Spirit.

Look at the next two verses in Ephesians 5:19-20:

Speaking to yourselves in psalms and hymns and spiritual songs, singing and making melody in your heart to the Lord; Giving thanks always for all things unto God and the Father in the name of our Lord Jesus Christ;

That word *for* should actually be *in*. "Giving thanks always *in* all things." In the past, you may have heard this taught, "Well, if I just start dancing around and am thankful to the Lord and make a melody to Him in my heart and sing a few psalms and a hymn here or there, then I can get filled with the Spirit."

But I think that's a bit backwards. I think singing songs and making melody in your heart is actually evidence as to whether or not you are filled with the Spirit. If you're filled with the Spirit, you will be making melody in your heart to the Lord. You will be so thankful you can't stand it. You'll speak in line with the Word of God and run around with a melody deep in your heart that no one can take away from you. That's the indication to you that you are filled.

Why is this important to know? Because the only time you can rely on your decision-making process is when you're making melody in your heart to the Lord and you're thankful to Him. That's when you are filled with the Spirit, speaking revelation from the Lord and understanding His will. If you're feeling disgruntled, oppressed, whiny, or uptight, you are guaranteed to make a bad decision.

For some people, that means they'd never make any decisions. The frown on their faces is a permanent fixture; they walk around thinking, speaking, living with a pessimistic outlook on life. But they can change. It starts by being continually filled with the Spirit. When you're filled with the Spirit, the frown has to go. You can't help but be happy.

This is just another way to look at the decision-making process. When we're filled with the Spirit, we're filled with the understanding of the will of God. If we're filled with the understanding of the Word of God, our decisions will be good. Our indicator that we're filled with the Spirit is that we're making melody in our hearts and thanking God.

THE ESSENCE OF BEING FILLED

You cannot be filled with the Spirit without a conscious overriding awareness of His presence in your life. I'm not sure which comes first—being filled with the Spirit is what makes you

Be Filled With the Spirit

conscious of God or being conscious of God is what opens you to the fullness of the Holy Spirit.

They probably go hand in hand.

Your recognition of His indwelling presence is what enables Him to get big in you. When you recognize that Jesus never leaves you or forsakes you, when you realize that He is closer than your skin, when you realize that God is with you all the time, your outlook on life is transformed. You won't look at life through the eyes of defeat; you'll see things through the eyes of the Greater One inside you.

This is the essence of being filled with the Spirit: You think about Him. You talk to Him. You are consciously aware of His presence.

We come to church and say, "Oh, Lord, pour out Your Spirit." But Jesus already said, "For where two or three are gathered together in my name, there am I in the midst of them" (Matthew 18:20). He's already there. It's time we start believing what He said.

You are filled. If you've been baptized with the Holy Spirit, you've been filled and put on fire for the Lord.

It starts by believing it, and then being aware of it.

A lot of elements heighten your awareness of His presence. When you spend time in prayer, directly communing with the Lord, your awareness of Him will be strengthened. Practicing the presence of God is, in a way, a form of prayer. When you walk through your day and you're communing with God by your awareness of Him, and you run into a problem with your banker, the first thing you'll do is talk to the Lord. "Lord, didn't you say...?" You'll ask Him for wisdom and guidance. And then you'll call your banker.

If the Lord is absolutely the biggest thing in your mind, then you'll have a melody in your heart. You'll be thankful to Him.

You'll walk with a spring in your step, speaking psalms and hymns throughout your day. In that condition, everything in your heart is a revelation of the will of God. Why? Because you're filled with the understanding of His will.

If you're in that place in the Lord, you'll walk out of your prayer closet in the morning fired up enough to chew up logs and spit them out! You're just so happy you can't wait to see what God has for you today because you know the things He's shown you are going to unfold in your life. Absolutely every decision you make out of this place is going to be directed by God.

But you've got to believe it.

Being filled with the Spirit with the evidence of speaking in tongues is the number-one weapon against depression. If you're a Spirit-filled Christian, there's no reason for you to ever be depressed because you can pray in the Holy Spirit until depression has to leave. You'll be edified and built up, according to the Word. And as you're filled with the Spirit, you're making melody in your heart, thankful unto God. You can't stay depressed.

That brings me to a very important point. If tongues is the evidence of the initial filling, it only makes sense to carry that a little further and say it's one of the ways you remain filled. Because when you pray in the Spirit, you acknowledge His indwelling presence. That enables Him to rise up within you. It causes you to become more and more conscious of His presence throughout your day.

You can live this way—with an undercurrent of awareness of His presence and the power and anointing that He has brought to bear in you. That awareness can be in you even when you're at work, school, or home. No matter what your mind is doing throughout the day, an awareness of the Spirit can always be inside you.

That moment-by-moment consciousness together with your reliance on your Spirit-given prayer language will keep you filled.

The evidence will be a spring in your step, a melody in your heart, and a thankful attitude toward God.

When you're in this condition, you're safe to make godly decisions.

Confirming His Word

As you stay filled with the Spirit, there will be a knowing in you about what to do. The Bible calls it a peace or inward witness. That's just another way of saying you know the right way to go and which way to turn. You know what your response should be. That inward witness is your first clue as to how to respond to a decision you need to make.

God even goes further than that. In 2 Corinthians 13:1, He says that He will confirm every word that He has spoken to you in the mouth of two or three witnesses. God knows that the tendency of our flesh is to question whether or not we're hearing from God. He wants to put those questions to rest because the Word says that a wavering man receives nothing from the Lord (James 1:6-7).

God will bring two or three people by to speak to you in a way that will confirm what your inward witness is telling you. That doesn't mean you should try to figure out who He'll use or make demands on God. I have heard people say, "I believe God's going to confirm this through Brother So-and-so in a word of prophecy." Other people will say, "I won't act until I hear an audible word from my pastor."

That's a wrong perception of how God brings confirmation.

God often uses the people we least expect Him to use. He may use that person you snubbed at the front door this morning. Don't limit the people He can use to bring confirmations to you. This is one of the reasons it's so important that we keep our relationships right, grounded on the love of God.

Also, He will confirm His word in the mouth of two or three witnesses. He'll give you more than one, but not 15 or 20.

When you are filled with the Spirit, the peace inside you—your inward witness—will provide you with the direction for your decision making. God will then confirm His direction in the mouth of two or three witnesses.

AN OPEN DOOR

There's one other thing that has to be in place as you are Spirit-led in your decisions. What you do on the basis of what He has revealed and confirmed to you has to await providential circumstance. In other words, God will open a door for you to step through. Remember what Revelation 3:8 says? God will open a door that no man can shut. I briefly talked about this concept in chapter 17, but I want to expound on it.

Many folks get excited when they know the will of God about a situation in their lives; they feel a peace about what direction to go and God has confirmed that direction to them through two or three witnesses. But they don't consider the matter of timing. Usually they'll assume once God's direction has been confirmed, everything will happen right away. They'll think, *I'll start my new business tomorrow* or *I'll engage in this undertaking next week.* But even though a certain direction has been confirmed to you, you must wait for God's timing before you act. Let God open a door that no man can shut.

For instance, we started a magazine for our ministry over twenty years ago because I really wanted a magazine. I had seen it in my heart. I knew we were going to have a publication from this ministry. It was part of our vision, so I went out, hired people to do it, and scratched together some money which really wasn't available. The magazine didn't work.

One to two years later, God raised up somebody in the church who had a burning desire in her heart to put a magazine together for us. She was anointed and called to do it. Plus, we had the finances available to make it happen. The opportunity was there; this time, the timing was right for the magazine.

When God opens the door for something to happen, all the resources you need are available. That includes the people, the finances, the opportunities, the relationships—every detail is taken care of when you step out in God's timing.

Don't waste your time trying to kick down doors and make things happen. Don't let a delay make you question whether or not you've heard from God. We can't dictate the timing of things in our lives. God knows us. He knows what we need. He knows what we're prepared for. Even though I know we would like to help Him out sometimes, He doesn't need our coaching or our counsel.

Some things take a season to come to pass. Sometimes there are "suddenlies." I love "suddenlies." Whichever way comes to you, don't rush ahead of God. Whenever the doors open, they open. Until then, live your life as best as you can, knowing that His timing is perfect.

This describes a healthy approach to our daily decision making. First, be filled with the Spirit because then you will always know the will of God. Next, have faith in what you know. Remember when you're continually filled with the Spirit, you'll see the evidence by the melody in your heart and a thankful attitude to Him. Then God will confirm His direction to you in the mouth of two or three witnesses. Lastly, patiently wait until God opens a door for you to act.

I'm grateful that throughout this process, plenty of time is available for God to correct us if we need to be corrected. There have been a few times in my life when God corrected me. His correction often comes the same way. Perhaps you followed your flesh instead of your spirit, and made a wrong decision. Confirmations can then turn into corrections to turn you back toward the right path. God will make sure you get back on the path; He loves you enough not to let you fall off the edge of the cliff.

Each day you should wake up with this understanding; I know in my heart that I'm following the will of God because I'm staying filled with the Spirit. I trust my desires, my heart, and my inward witness. I've gotten confirmations and I know just like Elizabeth said to Mary, "There shall be a performance of those things which were told [you] from the Lord" (Luke 1:45).

You'll be walking in the perfect will of God for your life.

Epilogue

Properly controlling your soul is crucial to your life experience. Why?

Because your life will always be a product of the choices you make—and your soul is where you make your decisions.

When you receive Jesus as your Lord and Savior, your spirit becomes brand new, but your mind and body don't. Your mind needs to be renewed to the Word of God and your body needs to be disciplined. God gave you this responsibility, but He also provides you with the ability to do so.

The key to this process of transformation is gaining a working knowledge of how your soul—your mind, will, and emotions—operates.

Your soul is influenced by both your spirit and your flesh. The louder voice will win in your decisions.

The enemy labors to influence your flesh. He wants your flesh to produce a stronger influence on your soul so you can bring his will into the world.

God wants to influence your spirit through His Holy Spirit. As you choose to yield to His Spirit inside you, your spirit will have a stronger influence on your soul and you'll bring God's will into the world.

So, who is it that controls your soul?

Have you given the enemy control by yielding to your flesh?

Or have you followed your spirit and let the direction of the Holy Spirit rise up inside of you?

Remember, whoever controls your soul controls your destiny.

Prayer of Salvation

A born-again, committed relationship with God is the key to a victorious life. Jesus, the Son of God, laid down His life and rose again so that we could spend eternity with Him in heaven and experience His absolute best on earth. The Bible says, "For God so loved the world, that he gave his only begotten Son, that whosoever believeth in him should not perish, but have everlasting life" (John 3:16).

It is the will of God that everyone receive eternal salvation. The way to receive this salvation is to call upon the name of Jesus and confess Him as your Lord. The Bible says, "That if thou shalt confess with thy mouth the Lord Jesus, and shalt believe in thine heart that God hath raised him from the dead, thou shalt be saved. For whosoever shall call upon the name of the Lord shall be saved" (Romans 10:9,13).

Jesus has given salvation, healing, and countless benefits to all who call upon His name. These benefits can be yours if you receive Him into your heart by praying this prayer:

Heavenly Father, I come to You admitting that I am a sinner. Right now, I choose to turn away from sin, and I ask You to cleanse me of all unrighteousness. I believe that Your Son, Jesus, died on the cross to take away my sins. I also believe that He rose again from the dead so that I may be justified and made righteous through faith in Him. I call upon the name of Jesus Christ to be the Savior and Lord of my life. Jesus, I choose to follow You, and I ask that You fill me with the power of the Holy Spirit. I declare right now that I am a born again child of God. I am free from sin and full of the righteousness of God. I am saved in Jesus'

name, amen.

If you have just received Jesus Christ as your Savior, or if this book has changed your life, we would like to hear from you. Please write us at:

Mac Hammond Ministries
PO Box 29469
Minneapolis, Minnesota 55429-2946

You can also visit us on the web at
mac-hammond.org.

About the Author

 Mac Hammond is senior pastor of Living Word Christian Center, a large and growing body of Christian believers in Brooklyn Park (a suburb of Minneapolis), Minnesota. He is the host of the *Winner's Way* broadcast and author of several internationally distributed books. Mac is broadly acclaimed for his ability to apply the principles of the Bible to practical situations and the challenges of daily living.

Mac Hammond graduated from Virginia Military Institute in 1965 with a Bachelor's degree in English. Upon graduation, he entered the Air Force with a regular officer's commission and reported for pilot training at Moody Air Force Base in Georgia. He received his wings in November 1966, and subsequently served two tours of duty in Southeast Asia, accumulating 198 combat missions. He was honorably discharged in 1970 with the rank of Captain.

Between 1970 and 1980, Mac was involved in varying capacities in the general aviation industry including ownership of a successful air cargo business serving the Midwestern United States. A business acquisition brought the Hammonds to Minneapolis where they ultimately founded Living Word Christian Center in 1980 with 12 people in attendance.

After more than 26 years, that group of twelve people has grown into an active church body of more than 9,000 members. Today some of the outreaches that spring from Living Word include Maranatha Christian Academy, a fully-accredited, pre-K through 12th grade Christian school; Maranatha College, an evening and weekend college with an uncompromising Christian environment; Living Free Recovery Services, a state licensed outpatient treatment facility for chemical dependency; Club 3 Degrees, a cutting-edge Christian music club which is smoke/alcohol free; Living Word Compassion Center, a multi-faceted outreach to inner-city residents; CFAITH, an online cooperative missionary outreach of hundreds of national and international organizations providing faith-based content and a nonprofit family oriented ISP; and a national and international media outreach that includes hundreds of audio/video teaching series, the *Living Word Live* and *Winner's Way* broadcasts, the *PrayerNotes* publication, and the *Winner's Way* magazine.

Other Books Available From

By Mac Hammond

Angels at Your Service

Releasing the Power of Heaven's Host

Doorways to Deception

How Deception Comes, How It Destroys, and How You Can Avoid It

Heirs Together

Solving the Mystery of a Satisfying Marriage

The Last Millennium

A Revealing Look at the Remarkable Days Ahead and How You Can Live Them to the Fullest

Living Safely in a Dangerous World

Keys to Abiding in the Secret Place

Plugged In and Prospering

Embracing the Spiritual Significance and Biblical Basis for the Local Church

Positioned for Promotion

How to Increase Your Influence and Capacity to Lead

Real Faith Never Fails

Detecting (and Correcting) Four Common Faith Mistakes

Simplifying Your Life

Divine Insights to Uncomplicated Living

The Way of the Winner
Running the Race to Victory

Water, Wind & Fire
Understanding the New Birth and
the Baptism of the Holy Spirit

Water, Wind & Fire—The Next Steps
Developing Your New Relationship With God

Who God Is Not
Exploding the Myths About His Nature and His Ways

Winning Your World
Becoming a Person of Influence

Winning In Your Finances
How to Walk God's Pathway to Prosperity

Yielded and Bold
How to Understand and Flow With the Move of God's Spirit

By Mac and Lynne Hammond

Keys to Compatibility
Opening the Door to a Marvelous Marriage

*For more information or a complete catalog of teaching
CDs and other materials, please write:*

Mac Hammond Ministries
PO Box 29469
Minneapolis, Minnesota 55429–2946

Or visit us on the web at:

mac-hammond.org